The Angler's Bible

The Angler's Bible

Essential Tips for
Coarse Fishing

Colin Mitchell

NEW
HOLLAND

Published in 2015 by New Holland Publishers
London • Sydney • Auckland

The Chandlery Unit 9, 50 Westminster Bridge Road, London,
SE1 7QY, United Kingdom
1/66 Gibbes Street, Chatswood, NSW 2067, Australia
5/39 Woodside Ave Northcote, Auckland 0627, New Zealand

www.newhollandpublishers.com

A catalogue record of this book is available at the British Library.

ISBN: 9781742576787

Managing Director: Fiona Schultz
Publisher: Alan Whiticker
Project Editor: Angela Sutherland
Design: Andrew Davies
Production Director: Olga Dementiev
Printer: Toppan Leefung Printing Ltd (China)

10 9 8 7 6 5 4 3 2 1

Follow New Holland Publishers on
Facebook: www.facebook.com/NewHollandPublishers

Contents

Foreword

The best anglers learn from experience and from those who are naturally gifted when it comes to having 'fish think'.

You don't have to be super fit or train for days on end to become a top angler in search of big fish or match victories, but it does help if you have a sharp brain to remember everything you learn, and you are physically and mentally fit enough to put all of those skills into practice.

No book can teach you everything you need to know about fishing or how to be successful at the sport. But the information on the following pages should help you learn some new tricks to help you catch more fish.

All of the tips are valid in UK and European venues that hold these species, you may even think of ways of adapting them, for your favourite waters. Even pleasure anglers, who like nothing better than to sit in the peace and quiet of the countryside, can still use tips from big fish anglers and match anglers to help with their fishing – to catch more and bigger fish.

Whatever your style, everyone can learn something from these tips; even the best match anglers in the world admit they are still learning. Once you stop learning in competitive fishing you are on the way down.

The tips, tricks and experiences in this book have been built up over decades of fishing on a whole variety of waters in the UK and Europe. They have also been gleaned from fishing with and alongside some of the best match and pleasure anglers in the world. And there are some special features from some

A lovely sunny day, an unspoiled lake and a nice fish... it doesn't get much better!

Colin Mitchell with a nice pole-caught common carp.

Fishing gets you away from it all...peace, pleasure and seclusion.

top match and big fish anglers, aimed at getting you to think more about your fishing which in turn should lead to you catching more.

My thanks to the guys who helped me out with these features; they are proof that most top anglers are so passionate about their sport that they are more than willing to offer advice.

The only way to get better at your fishing is to keep learning. You will learn from experience, but you will also get an awful lot of information from top anglers if you watch them carefully and ask them politely what they are doing.

I hope this book gets you thinking about what you are doing, helps you get more bites and more fish... and appreciate even more the great scenery, camaraderie and enjoyment that angling brings to millions of people around the world.

Colin Mitchell
Spring, 2015

Chapter 1

The Right Stuff

1.1 Rods and reels

There is a vast choice of rods and reels available today to cover virtually every aspect of angling, and the good news is that much of this hardware is now a lot cheaper than it was a decade ago.

Top of the range tackle is expensive and in many cases still very desirable. But even budget priced gear can give many years of good fishing and would not be out of place in a top angler's holdall or seatbox.

Set out below is just a very basic guide to what to look for when buying a rod and reel.

Your final choice is best guided by listening to other anglers who have used the various kit you are considering, closely examining reviews of the gear by testers and, most of all, finding out how the gear performs in your own hands.

What feels good to you will make you fish better. But you will also know better than anyone if the rod and reel is up to the job that you will most use it for.

Rods

Don't be fooled into thinking that there is such a thing as a good all-round rod. You want a totally different tool for float fishing than you do for legering and swim feeder work.

Check the rod has good rings. You want line to go through them easily for good casting and ideally they should be hardened or contain a lining so that continued friction from line doesn't wear them down too fast. Thin wire rings that bend very easily should be avoided.

Most rods now come with screw up or down reel fittings. Don't settle for less, you don't want your reel to drop off the rod as you play a good fish!

Check ferrules fit snugly. Reject a rod that has big gaps between the sections when the ferrule is fitted together.

Cork or Duplon are the main materials for handles and both are satisfactory, although cork has the edge as a material of choice. Avoid plastic. Some specimen rods have abbreviated hand covering, which is no problem at all.

Handles will vary in length, check that the one on your chosen rod feels right and that it isn't too short or too long. A rod should feel like an extension to your arm.

Float

For most general float fishing an 11-, 12-, 13- or 14-foot-long rod will do the job. Most anglers settle for a 12 or 13 footer. A fast tip action will help you pick up line quicker with a nice sweeping strike, but you need backbone down the centre of the rod to land big or hard fighting fish.

Many rods nowadays have a good progressive action that gives them a soft forgiving feel when you first hook a fish or when you get a smaller specimen. Then, as a fish runs hard and you hold on, the power of the rod kicks in but is still forgiving enough so that your hook doesn't pull out of the fish's mouth or the line snaps with a sudden jerk – something that you get with a rod that is simply too powerful.

Check what the manufacturers' suggestions are for the rod. They will often say what sort of float fishing the rod is for whether it be waggler, pellet waggler or a power rod for big floats. Also note their suggested line ratings – most now indicate the heaviest reel line and recommended traces you should use. However, they are only a guide, not a hard and fast rule.

Leger/Feeder Rods

There is a huge range of rods available for both straight legering and swim feeder fishing.

The principles of what to look for in terms of rings and reel fittings are the same as float fishing. A light legering rod will not be built to handle the regular casting and retrieval of a decent sized swim feeder. It

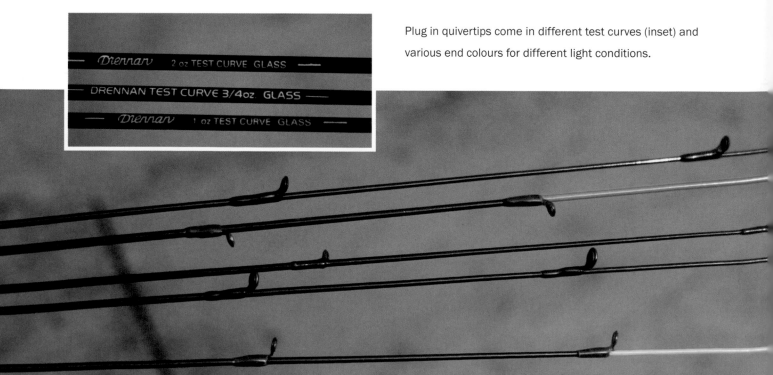

Plug in quivertips come in different test curves (inset) and various end colours for different light conditions.

may cope with a small feeder over short distances but it is not designed for this purpose.

Rods designed for feeder fishing are often rated as light, medium and heavy/distance. A light or medium version could cope with straight legering and light feeder work if you can't afford more than one rod for this type of fishing.

A key element to consider for any of the above rods is the quivertip – the end section that registers the bites. Some of the lighter rods come with one or two tops that have the quivers built into them. These are often very specialist tools and don't really give you the option of using them for anything other than what they were built for. Ideally you want a rod that has plug in quivertips. This allows you to change your tip to suit conditions.

Quivers can come in different lengths but mostly they are rated in test curves that range from a very sensitive half-ounce for shy bites up to three or even four ounce tips for rivers or bigger fish.

Quivertips are made from either glass fibre or carbon. Glass tips are by far the more sensitive and popular, although carbon tips do have their uses –

mostly in conditions when you need a top that offers a bit more resistance, such as faster flows.

The ability to buy extra quivers to replace broken ones or change the test curve to suit your fishing on any one-day is a massive bonus.

Specimen

A rod often referred to as an Avon – because it was commonly used on the famed Hampshire Avon for big fish – is the preferred tool for many specimen anglers when float fishing.

Ensure rods have quality rings

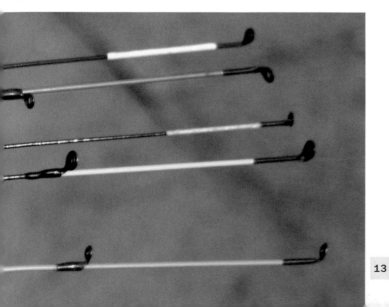

It is basically a stepped-up version of a float rod to deal with heavier tackle and bigger fish. Some anglers also use one of these for legering when after bigger fish.

Even though most rods will have a stated test curve, it is big fish anglers who tend to use this rating more than any other section of the sport as a better guide when choosing their preferred tackle for specimen hunting.

The test curve has nothing to do with the size of fish that the rod can land. Even the smallest test curve can land a massive fish without snapping! A test curve is the rating a rod gets when a weight makes the rod bend at 90 degrees. So if a 1lb weight takes a rod to that angle, 1lb is its test curve.

But don't assume that a rod with a 1lb test curve with be less powerful than a tool with a 2.5lb test. More times than not the heavier test will be the stronger rod, but you must also take into account how the full rod reacts when playing a fish.

A tip-actioned rod with a 1lb rating may pull round to its test curve quickly and then have backbone to really bend into a fish. A rod with a 2.5lb test might not have power through its middle and down into the butt.

Before buying ask about the full power of the rod. Make sure you buy one that isn't too weak for the fish you are after – but also ensure that it isn't too powerful either!

- Tubes often come with plastic caps to prevent rods falling out. Put a small hole in the cap and another small hole at the top of the tube and use a length of string through each hole so that the caps don't get lost when you open the tube.

Fixed spool

Reels

Fixed spool

The most popular kind of reel that is easy to use, a fixed spool casts easily and comes in a variety of sizes. Most reels from the major manufacturers, and nowadays even some of the models from lesser-known makers, are up to the job. It is usually the case of the more you pay the better the model you buy, especially with the big name brands. But if the reel has quality ball bearings, a good gear ratio, a spare spool and a roller of some kind on the bale arm you can't go far wrong.

You also need to check if the reel has an anti-reverse and a clutch – most reels have both! The clutch is used to tighten or release line pressure when playing a fish and is either front or rear mounted. Both have their advantages and at the end of the day it boils down to personal choice. Better gears and some of the bonus features offered by top makers – such as anti-wobble or better line lay – are all worth having.

Gear ratio is judged on how many times the spool turns for each turn of the handle. A reel with a gear ratio of 6:1 means that every time you turn the handle the spool turns six times. The lower the ratio the slower

the reel. But don't think you need a faster reel for every job – a slower ratio reel can be better for retrieving heavy weights. And don't think a bigger ratio reel will actually retrieve line faster – that will also depend on the size of the spool. The bigger the spool the more line retrieved.

Some reels come with double handles and a number of anglers find these are easier to grab when starting to reel in – and that they can offer better balance. They are more of a preference than a necessity.

Closed face

A closed face reel is a fixed spool reel but with the spool enclosed in a casing. These used to be very popular for float fishing but not so much nowadays. In wild, windy conditions closed face reels are brilliant, as

Closed face

Centrepin

line does not get blown off the spool or into tangles. And as they are generally smaller than normal sized fixed spools it is a lot easier to kept your finger on the line to control its flow off the spool in running water.

The biggest drawback to closed face models is that if you hook a big fish the line can bed into the line already on the spool as you reel in, which hinders casting afterwards.

The closed face reel is also a very handy reel if you are float fishing at medium range on rivers and for small to medium sized fish. Some models do not have anti-reverse or a clutch, so it is a case of backwinding – which many anglers do anyway – if you do end up playing a bigger fish.

Centrepin

The original reel used by anglers based on a large, free running drum, the 'pin has seen a resurgence in popularity in recent years.

A centrepin is not so easy to cast with but once you master the trick of pulling line off the drum with your fingers placed between the rod rings this really is fishing at its best.

A 'pin gives you great control over a float in running water and also helps when you are playing a big fish, allowing you to use your finger on the drum like a break. You really are in direct contact with the fish.

Centrepins are also great on still waters, especially when fishing down the margins for big fish. When specimens run they can take line very quickly and the 'pin allows you to let them run with less fear of breakages whilst still retaining control.

Multiplier

Multipliers were always regarded as a sea angler's tool but anglers seeking big pike and zander have recently adopted them, for both trolling and fishing live and dead baits.

These reels are definitely for the specialist angler as they are not easy to cast and, with the exception of the above uses, they have limited value to most freshwater anglers.

TIPS

- Try to buy a reel that offers you at least one spare spool. If it doesn't, check that spools are available and how much they cost.

- You don't have to put hundreds of yards of line on your reel just because the spools will take it. Many anglers look for a shallow spool or use backing – something like old line or sticky tape – to fill the spool to a manageable depth before adding new line.

- Don't put too much line onto a centrepin, only put on how much you think you may need. Line will then come off the drum a lot easier, you will be able to run a float through fast water without bumps and playing a big fish will also be a lot smoother. Too much line and it will bed in on itself and can come off the spool in jerks.

- Make a point of cleaning reels on a regular basis as dirt and groundbait can get stuck to them and affect their performance. Just rub down with warm water containing a bit of washing up liquid and maybe a quick squirt of WD40.

- Be careful when using fast retrieve reels – the speed can cause your end tackle to spin like a propeller and cause line twist. Many anglers incorporate a tiny swivel into their set up to help prevent this – even when float fishing.

- You can play a bigger fish either by back winding the handle or on the clutch/drag. It is still best to set your drag so that it gives line before your trace snaps. Adjust the drag before you start to fish and then you won't get caught out by a big fish that suddenly tears off when it is hooked and gives you no chance to backwind.

- It's easy to forget what breaking strain line or braid you have put onto your reel. Some reel spools now come with push-in plastic buttons that carry numbers that depict breaking strains. If your reel does not have these, mark the strain inside the spool with a marker pen – or put on a small sticker, write on the strain, and then cover with a bit of clear tape so that it does not get washed off.

- Always try to balance the weight and size of your reel to the rod you are using – small reel for a light short rod, bigger, heavier duty reel to a longer, heavier rod. It might sound obvious but many anglers under or over-gun their rods. If you are using a stronger rod you must be fishing for larger fish – so a bigger reel with extra power makes sense anyway!

1.2 Pole fishing

Pole fishing is relatively easy to learn, and certainly a great way of presenting a bait accurately.

The key to successful pole fishing is not to try and fish past the length at which you feel comfortable. And don't use a pole when a rod and line would be much better for the job!

A pole will allow you to fish a lighter rig than you would need on rod and line because you don't have to cast – you lay the rig on the water or lower it into your swim.

The pole also allows you to get up close to features like trees, islands and weed beds without casting into them as you could with a bad cast with a rod.

You can also accurately plumb the depth around your swim looking for shallow and deep areas that could hold the fish better depending on the conditions.

With the tackle now available most anglers can afford a reasonable length pole. But there is no point

Let your elastic do its job when playing big fish on the pole.

buying a 16-metre-long (52-foot-long) model if you are never going to use it at that length.

You would be far better buying a shorter pole with the same cash – which would probably give you a much better piece of gear.

Many anglers can fish comfortably at 9, 10 and 11 metres (30, 33, 36 feet) and, if you think about it, this is quite often the maximum distance at where fish live in many venues. A lot of the time the margins are the best spots of all!

And when you are faced with a big open water where the fish are at distance your pole should stay in its bag and the rod and reel should be out.

Selecting a pole

It's virtually certain that buying a good pole will be the biggest single investment you make in a piece of fishing tackle.

For that reason alone it is important that you make the right choice. It's going to have to last you for a time and the resale value will be significantly lower than what you bought the pole for, even if it's a top-

Nose cone (left) to protect joints and skid bung to protect the butt section of poles.

of-the-range piece of kit. The best guideline is: buy what you can afford but go for the longest pole you are likely to use. There is no point buying a 6-metre (20 foot) model if you are going to fish anywhere other than the margins. Likewise, what is the point in buying 16 metres (52 feet) if you never want to fish

Poles can reach tight spots you couldn't cast into.

Plummets are vital to find the right depth. A large one (left) for deep waters and hard bottoms, a smaller one for softer beds on waters.

Special brushes can be bought to clean the insides of pole sections.

at that distance? The shortest length to consider is around 11 metres (36 feet) – especially if you can buy additional sections to give it more length at a later date. But with lower prices it's well within reach of many anglers to now buy a pole of 12.5 metres (41 feet) or even 14 metres (46 feet). Don't buy long just because the price was right. You have to be able to fish with this piece of kit – it can't be too top heavy at its longest length, and you also want it to be reasonably stiff.

You also want a good package of spares. It should come with more than one top kit – two is good, three or more even better. Some top manufacturers guarantee that pole sections will be available for a number of years after the pole has first hit the market. Check if this is the case with the model you fancy. There's no point shelling out, accidentally breaking a section and then finding after a few months that there are no spares available. Also check how much spares are going to cost! Some poles look a good deal until you discover that spare top kits and the thicker, lower sections will make your bank account shrink very fast.

Pots (left) clip on near the end of your pole and cups can screw into an adaptor on the end of a spare top section so that you can feed accurately.

TIPS

- Check joints for wear, build them up if they are going thin. Clean the insides – dirt can affect the action of a pole and will, eventually lead to wear you could avoid.

- Don't leave sections laying on the ground where bikes or passers by could easily walk on them.

- Check if other, cheaper top kits and spares will fit your pole. They may not be as good as original spares but a lot of what are termed universal sections can do the job pretty well.

- Telescopic poles have their uses, particularly when used as whips for fishing to hand but take-apart poles are the best for all round fishing.

- Fit skid bungs in the butt of your pole. Usually made from plastic, these fit the larger sections and help prevent them being broken or shattered when you feed back through bushes – or if you accidentally hit something else.

- Put nose cones on the joints. Some poles come with these already in place but you can buy plastic ones. They act as a guide so that your top section fits more easily over the bottom one without hitting it, thus reducing further the danger of accidentally breakage.

- You don't need to strike when pole fishing. Lift firm and positive to set the hook. Remember that the tip of your pole is a lot closer to the fish than if you were fishing a rod and reel.

- Always use a roller when pole fishing. Feed your pole back on the roller to prevent undue pressure on the sections which could lead to a break – and also to keep the pole from being scratched on rough ground or getting dirt in the joints. Do not be afraid to use more than one roller when you are fishing a really long pole – or even break down your pole more than once.

Side puller systems on a pole help you land bigger fish faster when using a lighter elastic. This means you are able to go for smaller and larger fish at the same time without fear of bumping off smaller specimens because your elastic is too tight.

- Keep the distance between pole and float tip to a minimum so that you can hit bites faster. An optimum length is around 30-45cm (12-18 inches) but go shorter when you want to put your rig tight to features like bushes. You can have longer lines between tip and float to fish to hand, or so that the pole does not blow around in the wind and pull your rig out of position.

- Back shot help hold your rig steady. Place small shot, or even larger ones in very windy and rough conditions, on your line above the float. This stops the line blowing about and being dragged out of place. On flowing water back shot help you hold the rig back and slow the bait down. These shot could be placed from just a few inches (around 5cm) to a couple of feet (60cm) above the float, depending how and where you are fishing.

- Make sure that your internal pole elastic is not too tight or you will bump fish off the hook. You want the elastic set so that it just creeps back into the pole tip after it has been stretched whilst playing a fish. If you

are fishing near snags or features for big fish you can tighten elastic – but remember also to step up the size of your hook and breaking strain of line or you will snap off on the strike.

- Accurate feeding is possible using a pole cup or pot. But remember that if you use a separate top for cupping in bait it should be the same length as the top carrying your rig. If a pot won't clip on to the very end of your pole because the tip is too thin put some electrician's tape around the pole to make the tip thicker.

- When you have plumbed up your pole rig and found how deep your swim is, mark the depth of the water on your pole with a marker pen that can be washed off, or use a small elastic band. You can put more than one marker on the pole if you are going to fish the same rig at different depths.

- Use a big plummet in deep, flowing water so that it gets to the bottom and you can keep a tight line. In lakes, where there is often silt on the bottom, use a lighter plummet or the weight will sink into the mud and give you a false depth reading.

- Keep pole joints clean and free of grit and they will last longer. If a section becomes loose you can buy special graphite sprays to build the joints up so that sections fit more snugly.

- If joints stick together, usually because they are damp or dirty, let them dry out. Another good dodge is to get a friend to help pull them apart – put one hand each on either side of the stuck joints and then pull straight. You will be amazed at how easily they sometimes come apart! Pull straight or you risk breaking sections.

- Whatever distance you fish with a long pole it is sometimes worth adding another section, even if it sticks out behind you. The extra weight of this section will help you balance the pole better in your hands and make in more stable.

- Never lift a long pole by having your hands closer to the tip than the butt. This is a sure-fire way of getting broken sections.

- If you are fishing and a section breaks don't despair. Push the top part of the broken section up through the bottom part and it will give you enough of a repair to carry on. Tape over the piece that is shattered – carbon splinters really hurt if you get them stuck in your hands or fingers.

- Every few months, or at the end of a season, clean your pole inside and out. You can soak it in the bath or buy special brushes that fit inside sections. You will be amazed how much mud and grit gets inside the pole and this can both damage it and affect its action.

- In clear water or bright, sunny conditions, remember that fish can see your pole's shadow – or it may glint in the sun – and it could spook them away from where you are fishing. Try fishing with a longer line than normal so that you can hold the pole tip away from the area in which you are fishing.

- Always try to shot down your pole floats so that just a pimple of the tip is showing. You will be amazed at how you many bites that didn't appear when you had a lot of the pole bristle showing above the surface, now begin to register.

- If you have trouble shotting down your pole float and it hangs just below the surface, try greasing up the bristle. Use special pole float bristle which you can buy, or just a small smear of Vaseline.

- Always use three pieces of silicone to attach your line to the stem of your pole floats. This ensures the line is held flush to the surface of the stem and also means you have a spare to slide up or down, should the piece under the body or at the very end of the stem breaks.

- Be careful when you adjust the depth you are fishing at when you use wire stemmed pole floats. Slip the rubbers to the top of the stem, or right off, or you risk bending the wire.

1.3 Line and hook choice

One of the first things you do when you get to the water's edge is decide what strength (or diameter) of line you are going to use and what size hook will be tied to it.

The common belief is that light lines and small hooks equal more bites, whilst heavier lines and bigger hooks mean less bites but more chance of landing the fish. That generalisation is always the case. In haste to get a few more bites anglers often unnecessarily risk losing their prized captures.

Instead of thinking how small and light to fish, think how heavy can you go and what size hook will you get away with and still be able to get bites. It's good to get bites and hook fish but a waste of time if you lose the fish. It's also a waste of time sitting on the bank and failing to get bites.

The obvious answer is to change hook and line sizes if you lose fish or can't catch. But how many anglers actually make those changes? Or more important, how long do they take to make them?

As a general guideline you should match hooks and line to the size of fish you are after and the swim you are fishing. Clearer swims can handle light gear, snaggy areas need heavier – and you will get away with it because fish are more confident with those snags around.

Balanced tackle is vital. Pair light lines and small hooks with rods that are forgiving – those that are not as stiff as pokers and bend nicely into fish. On the pole, line and hooks need to be balanced to the elastic you are using, whether that is solid or hollow. Hollow elastic costs more but is definitely more beneficial and will helps you land more fish, especially if used with a puller bung. Hollows stretch more and as they stretch more – that is with bigger fish – they tighten up better. And if they don't tighten enough use the puller bung! They are great when you expect to encounter both big and small fish. There's no hard and fast guideline to what line to use, but remember that you don't need to use a 4 lb (1.8kg) breaking strain line to land a 4 lb (1.8kg) fish!

You might need heavy gear in snaggy swims but most of the time balanced tackle and playing skill will land fish much bigger than the breaking strain of your line.

Need proof? Tie a 1 lb (450g) trace to the end of you gear, loop it over a fence post and then keep pulling your rod back until the line snaps. It won't break as easily as you think!

If fish are shy biters and the water is clear, scale down on line diameter. When they are feeding well or there is colour in the water, step up the gear.

Hooks are a lot easier to sort. You can't get much more than one, maybe two, maggots on a 20 hook. An 18 is ideal for two.

Match the bait to the hook size. Don't struggle with a lobworm on an 18 – get those size 12s or even 10s out. Don't try to fish a piece of meat on an 18 – you can bury a big hook even in a small cube of meat. And don't forget that all sizes and types of baits can be hair rigged if you want to use a bigger hook with a smaller bait.

Still not sure? Ask anglers who are catching nearby what end gear they are using or experiment yourself. The best anglers in the country don't always fish light and small – in fact some fish heavy and big and get the results.

Fishing is about confidence, feeding and presentation. And sometimes presentation on the right hook and line will win you a lot more bites than even the best of baits.

Trace lengths

How important is the length of your hook length or trace?

A lot of anglers on commercial fisheries might admit to not using weaker links between their main line and hooks so as to avoid weak spots. But the space between their last shot and the hook, or between the hook and a ledger or feeder, is then the vital distance. There is always an optimum length and it will differ by the day. Using a trace of around 3 feet (91cm); if you miss bites – usually on the drop, despite fishing a heavy feeder – reduce this to around 18 inches (45cm) and you will probably get a few more fish. If they are deeply hooked, take it down a few more inches and you could find you hit a lot more bites and every fish is neatly hooked in the top lip.

It can be amazing how just a small adjustment can make so much difference. Don't just go shorter, try longer too until you hit most bites and the hook is neatly in the fish's lips.

Think of it a bit like shotting down your float so that a fish can pull it under easily. Just because a fish takes a feeder-fished bait doesn't mean it is any more stupid than one caught on a waggler or pole rig. Adjustments must always be made to get the best bite detection. Just remember to keep your hook bait close to the free feed coming out of the feeder, but at the same time you want to pick off fish that see the bait falling naturally. Obviously, if the fish are feeding on the bottom it doesn't matter so much about seeing it drop slowly through the water – but you still need to see bites quickly and as positively as possible.

Feeder fishing doesn't mean tying on a method rig. And in my book there should be no fixed rigs or self-hooking rigs – and certainly not when there are big fish about, unless you have taken precautions with weaker traces and/or links to weights and feeders.

If you are not sure about the best length of trace, start long and reduce by a few inches (5cm) until you get or hit bites properly. Likewise, it pays to experiment sometimes with the size of hook. Match hooks to baits but be prepared to step up a hook size or two. Small hooks do not always give you the same hooking power, especially at distance. I always used to start with a small hook and go bigger the more bites I got. Now I do it the other way around – safe in the knowledge that if I do get a bite I will probably hit it and then land the fish on the bigger hook.

The same rules apply when float fishing: get that last small shot on your line as near to the hook as you possibly can. Quite often the last shot can be just 3 inches (7cm) from the hook and, if the fish will accept that without ejecting the bait immediately, then you are on a winner and will hit bites fast and efficiently. Again, experiment by carefully moving the shot closer and further from the hook.

- Nylon line will last a very long time but make sure you do not leave it in direct sunlight – this can make it deteriorate faster.

- After every fishing trip, or before a new one, run your fingers over the last few yards of your line. If it feels rough cut it off the spool, as it may have been dragged over rocks and been weakened.

- If your line snaps during a session and you tie it back together, get rid of that length when you get home, even if it means putting totally new line on your reel. Knots can be a weakness and will certainly restrict casting ability.

- Many anglers now talk about line in diameters rather than breaking strains. The thickness of the line can be vitally important in getting bites. Thinner diameters can mean more bites.

- Traces, the length of line between your reel line and hook, can be any size from a few inches (5cm) to a couple of feet (around 60cm). They are important to help prevent losing tackle as they will snap first if you get snagged – but they also allow fish to break free without towing away end rigs. Fish can lose barbless hooks.

- Shock leaders, made from line a lot stronger than that on your reel, mean you can fish a lighter reel line. They are tied to your end rig, then go down your rod and go a couple of times around the reel spool. The

Don't just pick a line for its stated breaking strain – check the diameter too.

leader means you can cast a heavy rig without fear of snapping – and lighter/lower diameter line comes off your reel spool smoother than heavy line.

- The colour of line has been the subject of much debate and whether fish can see it. Some anglers use black, red or even yellow lines without much detrimental effect. A good guide is to maybe use clear mono when possible or even to match the colour of your reel line to the bed of the water you are fishing. The most important line in terms of colour and diameter is your trace.

- There are floating and sinking lines – make sure you have the right one for the type of fishing you are doing. You don't always want a floating line for float-fishing, though. When waggler fishing you will quite often want to sink the line.

- Be careful when you put new line onto your reel. If you take it off the plastic spool the wrong way, you can end up with massive line twist. If your reel's bale arm rotates clockwise, which is normal, then your new line must come of its own spool anti-clockwise. Always load line onto a reel the opposite way to which the bale arm rotates to stop line twist.

- If you do suffer line twist you can get rid of it with a simple method. Put a stone in a PVA bag – one that dissolves in water – then tie your line to this bag. Cast this as far as you can, wait for the bag to melt and lose the stone, then reel in. You may have to hold the line next to your rod to keep on some pressure but as you reel the twist will work its way out of the line.

- Just because your reel says it will carry hundreds of metres (say 220 yards) of line doesn't mean you have to use that much to fill it up. You can put some old line on first to act as backing – or leave some of your old line there when putting on new. That way it will cost you a lot less to fill the spool!

Hooks

Hooks are one of the most important parts of an angler's armoury – they come in many shapes and sizes but the basic requirements you should be looking for are always the same. You want a hook that is sharp, can handle the fish you hook and is big enough – or small enough – for the bait you are going to use.

There are thousands of hook patterns. Select the right one for the size of fish, type of fishing and size of bait.

The two basic patterns are spade end and eyed, which come in either barbed or barbless. Spades are more difficult to tie to your line but with a bit of practice this becomes easy and in many cases you will get better presentation. Eyed hooks can be tied in a number of ways, are great for beginners for that reason, and also offer a number of benefits you can't really get with spade hooks. Nowadays the knotless knot is one of the most important around for anglers who use eyed hooks and gives them the chance to tie hair rigs. Spade ends need to be checked to see they are not too big or the spade will spin in the water and give you line twist. Eyes need to be examined to ensure there are no big gaps where the ring is formed for the eye. Some hooks are even made without a join where the eye is formed.

Hook points should be carefully checked. They should glide easily into a maggot without bursting the grub. Any doubt and you should change your hook. Many anglers also carry around a sharpening stone to use on hooks that may get slightly blunted when they hit rocks or underwater obstacles.

Once you get past those basic of hooks there are many patterns from thin wire through to strong forged hooks to cater for different species and different sized fish.

TIPS

- The most popular sizes of hooks for coarse fishing range from a tiny No. 24 up to a giant No.2. The biggest selling sizes of hooks are 18, 16 and 14. As you have noticed, size of hook gets bigger as the number gets smaller, and are usually evens. There are some brands that do sell odd numbered sizes – which are between their even numbered counterparts.

- Don't think that all hooks in the same stated size are actually the same size! They do vary slightly between patterns and manufacturers, so a 14 by one maker could be slightly bigger or smaller than a 14 by another manufacturer.

- Don't try to use a big hook with small baits or vice versa. And don't think that a small hook will not land a big fish – if it is a strong pattern with a thick wire gauge and your hook hold is good there is no reason why it shouldn't.

- There has been a lot of discussion over the years about whether barbed, micro-barbed or barbless hooks are best, or which are safest for the fish. The truth is that all of them work well and all can be removed safely from a fish's mouth by using a disgorger or forceps.

- Many anglers believe that barbless hooks strike home far better – and if you keep a tight line to the fish whilst playing it there is no reason why the fish should come off the hook.

- Micro-barbed hooks have a part to play when using live baits such as worms that wriggle a lot and can come off a barbless hook.

- There is also an argument that barbed hooks, because of the barb, cause a slightly bigger hole whilst playing a fish so they can come out easier.

- You can help to keep worms on a barbless by slipping a tiny piece of rubber band over the point of the hook after putting on the worms.

- If you do get a hook stuck in a finger and can't get to a doctor quickly, the best way of removing it is by snipping off the spade or eye and push it right through your skin. If you haven't had a tetanus injection for a few years, go and get one!

A magnetic hook box prevents spillages. Some come with special tweezers with which to pick up a hook.

- Prevent spilling your hooks out of packets and boxes by keeping them in a magnetic hook box. They stick to the bottom of this, even if it flips open, and can be picked out easily one at a time.

- Many modern hooks won't go rusty if they get damp but ensure they don't go like this by putting a grain or two of rice into your hook boxes. This absorbs the moisture and should be changed every so often.

- During a fishing session always check your hook is still sharp. Blunted hooks won't take soft baits like a maggot so easily – and can also result in missed bites and lost fish.

- If your hook gets bent out of shape whilst fishing don't just bend it back. Change it! Hooks bent back to shape will be weakened.

Striking problems

Ever wondered when you should strike to set your hook?

When the tip goes round or when the float goes under would be the more obvious answers – but these are not always the correct ones.

Hitting bites – or at least trying to hit them – is a problem many of us have faced at some time or another. Some anglers believe that if you strike at every dip and twitch or pulled home into every definite pull round you will get more fish. But striking at bites actually needs as much thought and experience as when to change your hook size, type of bait or line diameter.

The late, great England international Ivan Marks said that you don't strike at bream bites until the tip goes round and stays there. You sit on your hands to resist the temptation. He also advised using small hooks, often the smaller the better.

Both those pieces of advice appear to fly in the face of reason. But think about it. A small hook is more easily sucked in by a bream – and most other species – so you get a better bite indication. And as Marks rightly pointed out, once a good little hook gets a proper hold it is difficult to shift, whilst a larger hook can create a bigger hole during a fight and slip out far more easily. The key to hook size is to match it up with the bait you are using! Commonsense.

Bream can always be a bit finicky, but for other species and various baits you have to think differently about when you strike. Some top class anglers try to hit every little twitch and microscopic movement on their quivertips. So, think about this. When you get a chance, lower some baited hooks into the water and

Fish on – after getting the strike right.

watch fish take them. Many species mouth the bait and yet you will see no movement on your tip or even on a sensitive float. Now imagine you are fishing and can't see the fish. How many times have you gone to reel in and found a fish on the end or a bait that has been sucked? That's right – you have missed loads of bites that haven't registered, or at least you think they haven't. Some of the indications you think are bites may not be but the law of averages said you could catch more than most anglers if you strike at most knocks.

This why, when you are able to, you should dot a float down so that just a pimple of the tip sticks above the surface and you can just see it. You can sit with just a quarter of an inch (half a cm) of a pole float bristle showing and see nothing. Dot that float down to a pinhead that is barely holding in the surface film and you see bites. And don't think these delicate eaters are just small fish, sometimes they are specimens that just haven't wanted to move far once they have taken some food.

The same type of thinking also has to be applied to bait. Different baits are taken differently. Maggots need a pretty fast strike. Fish gulp or suck them and as they are small baits they are usually in fishes' mouths at the slightest indication. Whilst meat, despite being soft, is often mouthed, pushed about and taken slowly, so don't strike too quickly. Punched bread is usually grabbed fast (another small bait) but even flake can be wolfed down and it's often regarded as an instant bait. Fish suck on worms or nibble them bit-by-bit; you need to take time before striking.

One way that often prompts a better take is to cut a worm in two. Hook the two bits so there is one open end next to your hook's bend and the other is dangling.

It's amazing how often this little trick brings bites when all else fails and quite often better bites.

Chapter 2

Baits and Groundbaits

The vast array of baits and additives now available in many tackle shops could leave you confused. But they are great news for anglers who like to experiment – after all, one of those baits is going to be just right for your favourite venue or species.

Anglers are always looking for an edge in a match or just simply to lure a few extra or bigger fish. Yet despite the fact we've got a plethora of groundbaits, boilies and pellets available to us there always appears to be one or two occasions when we are not sure what to fish with.

A quick look around a local supermarket is like opening up a new bait shop to experienced anglers. Lovely looking liver dripping in blood, fish sauce in a bottle, prawns, breakfast cereal… all could catch fish. Then there is the more likely luncheon meat, always a firm favourite with anglers. Don't just cut it into cubes like other anglers, make some strange shapes that stand out, have some rough the edges, make baits that look like pellets. The options are almost endless.

Of course the supermarket fish counter with mackerel, herrings, sprats and the like has always been a favourite for pike anglers, and for those seeking predators like eels and catfish. And sweetcorn is the No.1 bait for summer on many venues… but those nice green peas could be worth a try too. Roach are known to love them!

Maggots

Anglers always used to prefer big, fresh maggots. Now dead maggots have become a favoured feed and hook-bait. You can spot a fresh maggot by its size – large – and you will also see a black feed spot inside the bait if it is fresh.

Fish that are a bit wary will prefer a fresh hook-bait that is generally softer than older, tougher maggots. Older maggots can be good in winter as they do not stretch in cold water like fresh bait. Dead maggots should be freshly killed – or killed and then frozen until you use them. Some anglers scald maggots with hot water to kill them but just as efficient is putting them in a sealed plastic bag with the air removed. Maggots can last quite a long time with very little air and do not be surprised if the maggot you thought was dead comes back to life once exposed to the atmosphere!

Varieties

There are three basic types of maggot: normal big maggots, the smaller pinkie and the even smaller squatt. Big maggots are the most commonly used and pinkies, fished singly or as doubles, can be a great bait in winter or when fish are not feeding well. Don't think that because they are small they only lure small fish!

Squatts are sometimes used on the hook by anglers trying to catch small fish, or as loose feed on canals. They were also used in groundbait by bream anglers as this small bait does not crawl away into the bottom mud.

Double maggot. Careful how you hook them.

TIPS

- If your maggots start to sweat, get damp and smell like ammonia, put them through a riddle and place them in dry sawdust. You can also use groundbait but be careful this does not get wet, or it too will start to go sour.

- Change your bait with colourings. You can often buy maggots in colours such as red, yellow and the basic white but food colourings can give you different shades. Red has proved a very popular colour, especially when it is difficult to get bites. Change your hook-bait colour during fishing if bites dry up.

- Boost your baits with flavour. Many flavours, both sweet and savoury, can be bought in shops – but you can also use those sold in supermarkets for cooks and bakers. Don't add too much flavour – it can actually work against you and put the fish off feeding!

- Maggots can be hooked singly or you can put as many as you like on the hook, depending on hook size. Big fish anglers often use a maggot clip – a device like a ring that fixes to your hook and onto which you can thread a massive bunch of maggots to deter small fish from taking your hook-bait.

- Floating maggots can be used to counter balance the weight of your hook and make your bait look much more natural as it flutters through the water. To make a few maggots float, put them into a bait box containing just a shallow amount of water, which barely covers the grubs. The bait will take on air and after just a few minutes will float. Some anglers use fizzy drinks instead of the water, believing this also gives their bait a flavour boost.

Don't use rubbish bait – riddle your maggots so that you only get the good live ones (inset).

- When fishing two maggots, hook one at the blunt end, as normal, and the other by the pointed end. This should help prevent any line twist when you reel in. If you hook both grubs by the blunt end they can act like a propeller in the water. Don't burst the baits, ensure your hook is sharp.

- If you have trouble hitting bites – or even getting them – try pushing your hook slowly through the centre of the maggot and sliding it up the shank to hide the hook. Sometimes it can also pay to carefully hook the bait through the middle – you must use a very sharp hook and try not to burst the maggot.

Casters

Casters are the chrysalis formed as maggots turn into flies. A natural white maggot will first turn into a white, soft chrysalis shell and then move through shades of orange to reds and then go black before turning into a fly – a bluebottle in the case of normal big maggots. All of the different coloured shells can be used as a hook-bait, but loose fed casters should sink or they will tempt fish to the surface where they will swirl around eating the feed.

Casters can be fed loose or in groundbait and do tend to attract bigger fish than maggots. They are effective on all venues in both summer and winter. Once they have been mouthed by a fish the shells normally burst – and you should replace them.

TIPS

- Once your casters have reached the right colour you should riddle them off the maggots with a sieve and store them in a plastic bag containing a bit of air and inside a fridge. You can also put them in cold water to stop them turning further, but change the water at least once a day. Maggot riddles can be bought or you can make one with a wooden frame and the right size wire mesh that just allows lives maggots to crawl through the holes.

- Casters can be frozen but as soon as you take them out of the freezer put them in water whilst you are

Nice clean maggots.

fishing. Discard them at the end of the day as they should not be frozen a second time. Casters that go grey after this process should not be used – fish do not like them!

- All shades of casters can catch fish, depending on where you fish, what the fish fancy on the day and the species. White casters can often tempt big perch, the really dark ones that float often lure big roach. The floating caster counter balances the weight of your hook making the bait look much more natural to a fish.

- Do not feed casters as heavily as you would maggots. Some of the maggots will bury into the bottom – casters lay on the bottom until eaten!

- If fish are shy, bury your hook in the caster. Push the point through the blunt end of the caster and ease the hook gently into the bait, finally tapping the spade end or eye inside of the shell.

- Casters can be hooked just like maggots, in ones, twos or even more, providing your hook is big enough. When fishing double caster, put one up the shank and hook the other like a maggot. This helps prevent line twist.

- Loose fed hempseed is a great attractor, feeding just a few casters over the top of this and then fishing the shell on the hook. Try hemp on the hook later in your fishing session.

Nice fresh, damp worms – in this case dendrobaenas.

Worms

If you told experienced anglers they could have just one bait with which to go fishing, most of them would chose worms.

They are one of the most natural baits around, catch virtually every fish that swims, are available in most places and will work at any time of the year.

Varieties

Dendrobaenas

Dendras are the large worms most commonly bought from shops and worm farms. They are a hardy worm that will keep for some time – even months – providing they are not subjected to extreme heat or cold. A cool garage floor or a not too cold fridge is excellent for them. They are used a lot for chopping and quite often on the hook, but some anglers also like to have the two worms mentioned below for hook-baits.

Lobworms

The temptation is to dig these big juicy worms from your garden. But the much more efficient way is to find a damp piece of grass, in darkness, and just pull the worms out of their holes. Quite often you will find them laying on the surface – but you may have to move fast as they can be very quick! Use a shaded hand or head torch. These worms should be fresh, juicy and with their sticky outers intact for best results.

Lobbies can be great for all fish, but in particular for bigger specimens of chub, barbel, perch and carp. They are also excellent in flood conditions as fish are expecting these big worms to be washed down river in the extra water.

Redworms

These were often regarded as *the* bait for many fish, especially fickle feeding bream. They are the worms you will often find in compost heaps. They have natural appeal to fish – not only because of their colour but presumably because they are also very tasty! Rarely sold, you may have to find your own supply of this bait, or create a wormery in your garden using kitchen waste, such as raw vegetable peelings, lettuce and bread. They will breed well if you keep them fed!

Brandlings

These red-coloured worms usually have stripes or a saddle – a sort of band – around their bodies. They are slightly bigger than Redworms and look good on the outside, but many anglers do not like the yellow fluid inside. Usually found in dung heaps on farms and in the waste from stables they can still be an excellent bait for the hook or chopping.

TIPS

- Chopped worm fishing can be day-saver. When nothing else works a few worms chopped up and placed in your swim, followed by a worm on the hook, will often get a fish to feed.

- When you fish a worm over chop, keep yourself busy by slowly lifting and dropping your hook bait over the feed area or by dragging it backwards and forwards. This movement can make lethargic fish pounce.

- Two pieces of worm on the hook are often better than just one. Cut a worm in two and leave one of the open ends near the eye or spade of hook and the other open end away from it. Fish home in on the juice trail.

- Always nip the end off the worm on your hook to release a scent trail and to keep the worm lively. A dead and lifeless worm is next to useless bait!

- Worms transport well in peat but you can also use layers of damp newspaper, which tends to keep them fresh and appealing.

Pellets

Pellets for both feeding and using on the hook come in a variety of sizes and a whole range of flavours. The most common pellets are trout, carp and coarse, and each of these is available in sizes that range from micro up to 20mm – the biggest being for the hook.

Over the past decade pellets have become a very important part of anglers' bait armoury, used both as an attractant and on the hook. Fish-flavoured pellets, such as halibut, have been the most popular and often the most effective but now there are also a whole host of baits that use various marine flavours such as crab and krill plus many more sweet tasting baits.

Before investing in any pellets it is best to check the rules on the venues you fish. A number of fisheries now insist you use low oil content baits or even buy pellets that they sell on site. Some also impose a limit on how many kilos you can feed per session.

Hard pellets are the ones used mostly for feed and can be softened off by soaking in water for a short time. This also ensures that they sink when they are thrown in. Soft pellets are mostly for the hook. You can also buy expander pellets that need to go through a pellet pump to remove air and ensure they sink. These are great hook-baits that often catch when other baits fail.

Feed and hook pellets come in all shapes sizes and colours.

TIPS

● Hard pellets can be mounted on your hook by using a band. Some come drilled so that you can thread a hair through them and then use a custom-made plastic stop to keep them in place.

● Soft pellets often attract more bites but fall off the hook each time. Hard pellets might take longer to attract a bite but at least you know the bait will stay on longer and let you catch more fish before re-baiting.

● Pellets that have been well soaked can be moulded into a paste to put onto your hook. This can be a great hook-bait, especially to avoid small fish taking your bait.

● Specialist swimfeeders for feeding pellets are now available. These ensure that your hook-bait and free offerings are side by side.

- Method feeders, often used with groundbait, can also be filled with soaked pellets. Use a mould to ensure that the bait is firmly pushed in place and is also more aerodynamic than trying to create by hand.

- Feeding more than one size of pellet works well. But don't try throwing different sizes at one time – larger ones will go further than the small ones. If you are not fishing too far out it's worth feeding with a cup on the end of a pole.

- Remember that after they have been in the water for a time the pellets will become like small piles of groundbait. Keep feeding to keep fish interested, even if only six pellets every few minutes.

- The noise of pellets hitting the surface of the water can act as a dinner gong for fish! Carp especially have been used to finding food after hearing pellets hit the water – so make sure you keep bait going in.

- If you don't have a lot of pellets with you, try slapping your float rig onto the surface or hitting the water with your pole. The noise will again be associated by fish with food arriving.

- Normal practice is to feed pellets smaller than the ones on your hook so that your bait stands out to the fish. But smart fish might sometimes only take one size of bait. Experiment!

Meat

The most popular form of this fishing bait is luncheon meat, but anglers have also used the likes of steak, mince and liver to tempt prized specimens. Many anglers stick to one brand name of luncheon meat once they find a variety that works for them, but both cheap and expensive versions of this tinned meat will attract fish. Some anglers like to wash the bait before use, whilst others love to keep its various greases and natural elements intact.

Meat gives off a great smell in the water to not only attract fish into the swim but also entices them in to taking the bait on the hook. It can be fished in ragged pieces torn off the contents of the tin, cut into different shapes, cubes or even punched out into cylindrical pieces using a meat punch, which can be bought in good tackle shops. It pays to experiment with the size of meat you use on the hook and, as usual, match the bait to the size of the hook you are using.

Pieces of sausage, liver and bacon can all be used to lure various fish. A lot of river anglers used to

Meat is a good all-year bait. When you find a brand you like stock up with it!

loose-feed chopped up mince and fish a piece of raw bloodied steak on the hook. They had great results, especially for chub.

- Meat is a good all-round bait throughout the year for a variety of species, including carp, barbel, chub, tench, bream and roach.

- A piece of meat is a great attractor when a river is flooded and coloured, as the scent trail given off by the bait helps fish to find the food.

- A lot of novice anglers are worried that the soft meat will fall off the hook. The answer is to match the hook size to the piece of meat, or to hair rig the meat and make sure it stays on the hair by using a stop. There are specialist meat stops sold in tackle shops.

- Meat can be pushed through a riddle to form small pieces that can be fed loose or in groundbait. Groundbait can also be sprinkled on the meat to separate the pieces.

- Some anglers rub luncheon meat over a grater to gets slivers that can be fed loose. These flutter slowly through the water attracting the attention of the fish.

- You can also buy meat cutters that will dice the bait into cubes. Different sized cubes are cut depending on the cutter but the most popular sizes are 4mm and 6mm.

- Don't stick rigidly to cubes of meat on the hook. Fish can wise up to the same size if they see it often enough. Experiment with ragged edges, round pieces or even cutting the edges off cubes.

- Catfish, often linked with live and dead fish baits, love a nice big piece of luncheon meat. Some specimen anglers will use up to half a tin as one bait! Fish the bait on a hair rig.

- Frying luncheon meat for a short spell will put a skin on it and make it easier to keep on the hook.

- You can fry the meat with a touch of curry powder or other flavours to add a bit of an edge to the piece on your hook.

- If the meat hasn't been kept in warm and sunlight you can freeze it to use another day. If the bait has been exposed to heat for any length of time bin it!

- Liver used for bait should be raw. The blood from this offal helps to attract fish into your swim and can get them feeding too.

- Many top anglers feed cooked hempseed and just a few cubes of meat and then fish meat over the top. The hemp holds fish in your swim as they root around trying to eat it off the bottom – and doesn't feed the fish as much as piling in lots of meat.

Sweetcorn

One of the most natural baits around, sweetcorn was always associated with summer fishing until recent seasons. Now it is accepted as a good all-year bait that works well in many situations. In summer virtually all coarse fish will take a piece of sweetcorn – sometimes even more than one kernel on the hook is good, often to ward off the attentions of smaller fish. In winter, when the water is clear, many anglers do not feed corn – which is a very filling bait – but fish just one grain on a straight leger or float rig. The theory is that in the clear conditions fish, especially carp, can spot the bright yellow grains from quite a distance.

Corn can be put straight on the hook or it can be fished on a hair rig.

TIPS

● A number of baits can be fed when you fish corn on the hook. Groundbait, hemp, a few pieces of corn or meat, pellets – all can attract and the corn will certainly be the most visible!

● Most of the time you should hook the corn through the sealed end so that the open end of the kernel is showing. This is so the fish can see the tasty treat inside and it is where many fish will try to suck out the goodness.

● When the fishing is a bit harder try using half a kernel of corn on your hook – or even squeezing out the inside and just using the skin of the corn as your hook-bait.

● A good trick for feeding is to mash up a few grains of corn with scissors and add to your groundbait. Some anglers liquidise a bit of corn to add feed to their groundbait and give it a bit of extra taste.

● Never ditch the liquid the sweetcorn comes in. Keep the corn moist in it or mix to your groundbait for added flavour and to give it binding.

● Big fish anglers often use plastic corn as it looks just like the real thing and is not taken off the hook by small fish as they await the arrival of specimens. Dunk the plastic in some flavouring for a lengthy period before use to give it more appeal.

● You can buy sweetcorn liquid to boost your baits and groundbait. This has proven to be one of the best additives around.

● Sweetcorn is good to use in a cocktail bait. If you use a worm or maggots with it, put these baits on the hook first followed by the corn. The sweetcorn will help keep the live baits on the hook.

Sweetcorn is now no longer regarded as just a summer bait.

Boilies

Boilies are now one of the most important baits in an angler's bag, something that many take for granted. Yet it was less than 40 years ago that this bait first appeared, credited as the brainchild of carp angler Fred Wilton.

Carp anglers would be 'troubled' by other fish as they tried to track down their favourite species. They would often try unusual baits such as part-boiled potatoes to deter the other fish. But what they really wanted was a bait that would stay on the hook for casting to distance whilst at the same time attracting carp and able to resist attacks from fish like roach and small bream.

Using ingredients such as semolina and soya flour, mixed with various colourings and flavourings, the early pioneers used water or eggs to mix these items into a paste that was rolled into balls and then boiled for a short time in a pan of water. This created a skin on the balls of bait that became known as boilies. They could be cast out and left for long periods until the carp found the hook baits or until they needed changing because the flavours had leaked out totally. Many anglers started to make their own baits with variations on the ingredients and then a whole industry of bait makers surfaced offering hundreds of sizes, colours and flavours.

Bags of boilies are now commonplace in every fishing tackle shop and from their early beginnings in England the baits have appeared all over the world.

Varieties

There are many different sizes and flavourings of boilies. They are now available in tiny 4mm baits through to gobstopper-sized 40mm for bigger fish. There are standard boilies and buoyant boilies, which many anglers call pop-ups.

Flavours are usually split into sweet and savoury. These can range from pineapple through to crab, strawberry to liver! The list is almost endless as boilie manufacturers strive to find a new flavour to fool the fish – and these baits are no longer regarded as just for carp!

You can buy shelf-life baits that keep for ages, or freezer baits that need to be frozen because they contain no preservatives. Freezer baits are often thought to work better as they are frozen fresh and do not contain preservatives, but they do work out more expensive.

TIPS

- Boilies do not have to be fished whole! Quite often half a boilie can work – and some anglers cut one bait in two and then mount it on the hair rig with the flattened ends facing outwards. It looks different to wary fish and has the added advantage of leaking out smells better from the cut faces.

- Remember that boilies do eventually break down in water. When you reel in check that the bait will still withstand a strong cast or the attentions of smaller fish.

- Hair rigs are almost a must for boilies as the bait would mask too much of a hook point. But the length of the hair can be changed depending on how the fish are feeding. It can also be tied in a variety of ways (see opposite page for more details).

- You don't have to use just one boilie on your rig. Two baits will stand out more, especially if there are big fish around. Also you can use two different flavours or different sized baits to give you that bit extra.

- A 'snowman rig' incorporates both a normal and pop-up boilie on the hair. The smaller pop-up bait makes the set-up appear like a snowman as it sits on top of the larger bait and helps the bait stand up off the bottom of the lake. Carp can spot this more easily and can also take the bait easier too.

- If you make your own boilies do *not* be tempted to use more than the advised amount of flavouring. A bait may not smell much to you but a fish has a much more acute sense of smell than a human. A stronger smelling bait could actually deter the fish from taking it!

- Pop-up boilies can also be used as floating baits, fished with no weights on the line, maybe with just a controller float – to try and tempt carp from the surface.

- Normal boilies can be turned into floaters by giving them a quick whiz around a microwave oven. You can also carefully cut them open and insert a cork ball – or insert the cork when you roll your own boilies. You can also drill a hole in the boilie and insert a piece of rig foam.

Make your own

Many anglers like the convenience of buying boilies from a shop or picking up a packet of their favourite flavours.

But there is a lot of satisfaction in creating your own bait, selecting a flavour you think your quarry will like – and then catching on the boilies that have come out of your kitchen.

Here's a simple guide on how to make your own boilies…

Ingredients

8 oz (220g) soya flour
8 oz (220g) semolina
Two eggs
A flavouring – this could be a liquid or powder. You can buy one from a fishing tackle shop or have a look on the shelves of your local supermarket.

Method

1. Break the eggs into a bowl, add the recommended amount of flavouring (usually no more than two or three drops).

2. Add the soya flour and semolina slowly and keep mixing until you have a stiff paste. If it is too stiff you can add a touch of water or milk.

3. Roll the paste into balls, put it into a metal strainer and place into water that is already boiling on a stove. Remove after two to three minutes.

How to tie a basic hair rig

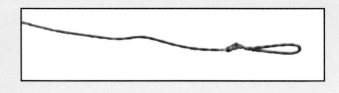

- Create a small loop at the end of your trace line.

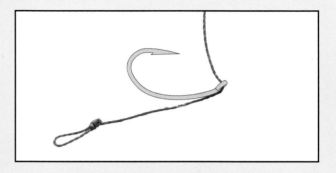

- Put your line through the eye of the hook so that the loop hangs down along the back of the shank. The loop should hang below the bend of the hook. This distance from hook to loop is judged by whether you want a long or short hair or the size of your bait – the bigger the bait the longer the hair.

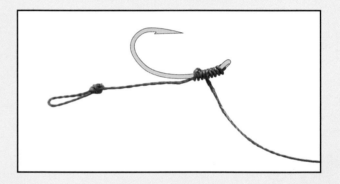

- Now wrap the end of the line opposite the loop around the hook shank around seven times, trapping the piece of line holding the loop against the wire. Keep your turns close together, like a nice rod ring whipping.

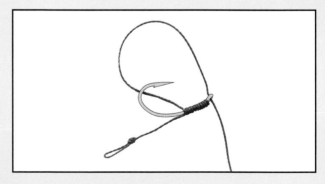

- Pull the loose end of line back through the eye from the back of the hook. Pull the knot tight and then your trace carrying the hair rigged hook can be attached to your main line.

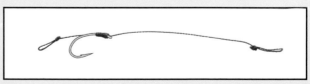

- Your bait is attached to the hair with the help of a baiting needle. The needle, which has a very small hook or barb, is pushed through your bait and then slipped into the hair loop. The needle is then pulled back through the bait until the loop is exposed. A small stop is pushed into the loop and gently pulled back to the bait. This stops the loop pulling out of the bait.

4. Tip the balls of bait onto a piece of kitchen towel to take off excess water. Your baits are ready to use – or can be put into a freezer bag and frozen until needed.

Pastes

Summer fishing for many anglers means using paste baits on the hook – although they can also be effective in winter!

This type of fishing originated when anglers used bread and cheese pastes on the hook for a variety of species. With the development of many commercial fisheries containing good-sized carp, bream, tench and crucian carp, paste has had a new dawn. Like boilies and pellets, pastes come in a massive range of flavours and can even be made at home.

Paste can be made simply by mashing up bread and mixing with water to form a mix that will stay on the hook. Cheese can be manipulated on its own to form a paste, or mixed with some bread. Even groundbait can be mixed into stiff balls to be moulded around a hook to use as bait. Basic boilie mixes form great hook pastes, although you obviously do not boil these baits in hot water.

TIPS

- Fishing paste means using a decent sized hook, no less than a 16 and usually a 14 or a 12 for bigger baits. You are hiding the hook so there is no worry about the fish being able to spot it.

- Most of the time you can mould paste around the bare hook ready to lower into the water. But sometimes it is worth having a pellet or piece of corn on the hook and mould the paste around this so there is something on the hook if the paste comes off. The bait on the hook also acts as an anchor for the paste.

- Remember that any paste that comes off the hook is like groundbait for your swim.

- Always try to adjust the depth of your float so the paste is just touching the bottom and keeps the tip of your float dotted down. Then if the bait comes off the hook the float will rise in the water. This could also be a bite, although more often than not paste bites are sailaways.

- Long tipped pole floats are great for this work – and of course you don't need a pole to fish a pole rig!

- Paste is often an instant bait so if you don't get a bite pretty quickly it is worth changing to another bait and going back to the paste later.

- Pastes will still work in winter but there is no doubt summer is best. Try a different flavour in winter – maybe a fruit one. Pastes can get hard in cold water and make it difficult to get bites and hook fish.

- Vary your paste hook-baits from the size of a pea up to the size of a meatball, depending on the fish you are targeting or if you want to avoid smaller fish.

- You won't hit every bite on paste – probably because in most cases the fish are sucking at it from a distance. Stick with the bait and with practice you will catch!

- Place the bulk of your shot just above your hook length or no more than 8 inches (20cm) from the hook. There is no need to fish paste so that it falls slowly through the water.

- A number of anglers use a float that is partially self-cocking and use the weight of the paste to dot down the tip. This way when the bait is either taken or falls off the hook the float pops up in the water.

- Making a paste bait is exactly the same as making the initial paste for a boilie (see boilie section). You do not need the eggs in the mix and do not need to put in boiling water.

Cheese

Once a very popular bait, many anglers now often overlook cheese, except for the dedicated specimen hunter. Regarded mostly as a chub bait, it will be taken by other species such as barbel, carp and tench.

The most popular forms are cubed pieces or a paste made from cheese or with some bread added. Either form can be used directly on the hook or fished on a hair rig.

- Strong blue cheeses can make excellent pastes. It is too soft to use in chunks on the hook.

- Rub cheese around in your hand until it goes soft and then you can mould it around your hook.

- Cheese is soft and can fly off your hook easily, so cast with care. In cold water the cheese will become hard so make sure you do not mask the point of your hook – and check the bait regularly.

- All cheeses will work as baits and it pays to experiment with the different colours and type of cheese you use.

Groundbait

Groundbaits are used to both attract fish and to act as a carrier for particles such as casters, hemp, maggots and all other hook-baits. There used to be a theory that groundbait led to the attraction of many small fish, but that is not always the case! And even if your groundbait does attract small fish, the activity from these could lead to larger specimens arriving to see what is going on.

Groundbait can be mixed differently to cope with different situations. You can have it active or inert. An active groundbait could be one that is mixed fairly dry so that it falls slowly through the water, creating a cloud and sprinkling food particles as it does. Or it could be a groundbait that goes to the bottom and then release active ingredients to get the fish moving around and chasing bait. Whereas, an inert mix goes straight to the bottom and stays there. This is when you want the fish to stay down and not rise in the water; when you want your free offerings to go down with the groundbait and create a carpet of feed for the fish to feed on.

Remember that an active groundbait can lead to a lot of fish in your swim which in turn could lead to line bites and foul hooked fish – which can come off the hook and scare away the rest of the fish in front of you, at least for a time. An inert groundbait could get the fish on the bottom and lead to less line bites or foul hookers – but it may also do little to attract the fish, unless they are inclined to feed. An inert bait is definitely better when the water is shallow and you do not want fish milling around in depths where they are more likely to catch your line.

As always in fishing it is a case of thinking about what is best on the day, for the conditions, the species you are trying to catch and the depth of water.

Varieties

The basic ingredient of most groundbaits is breadcrumb. But this can be coarse, fine, white, brown… as well as with many different additives are mixed in with the crumb to suit conditions and the species you are after. Sweet, fishmeal and savoury are often regarded as the three main areas for additives but different waters react differently and at different times of the years.

- You can ball in groundbait – that's throwing in a lot of balls, even as many as 12 the size of tangerines, as you start to fish. Quite often this noise doesn't scare away the fish but attracts them.

- The more usual way is to feed two or three balls of groundbait containing a few free samples of hook-baits and then top this up with smaller balls depending on the number of bites you are getting. Don't be tempted to put more bait in when the fish are feeding well. Many species – but especially bream – do not like groundbait falling on their heads.

- Don't think that groundbait always has to be fed in balls that go straight to the bottom. Try a ball that only just holds together and breaks up as it hits the water to form a cloud, or cup the bait in loose using a pole pot. The cloud will attract fish where they will feel safe.

- Dark groundbaits are best in clear water. They blend in better with the bed of the lake or river and fish are confident to feed over the bait as they know they wont be spotted over it by predators.

- If you are catching a lot of fish and want to keep them near the bottom make sure your groundbait is very damp – not runny, just very damp. You want every bit of it wet so that it sinks to the bottom. Any crumbs that have not fully absorbed water could rise towards the surface and fish would follow them.

- Don't mix live maggots in your groundbait! They will soak up water and float – they will also break up balls as you try to shape the bait. If you do want to feed live maggots in groundbait just add a few as you form a ball. Dead maggots are a good additive to groundbait.

- Keep a container of water next to your groundbait. This can be used to clean your hands – but if you also wet your hands before forming a ball of groundbait you will find this task easier, and the damp will put a nice glaze on the ball to prevent bits of bait dropping off.

Nice flavours

Here are a few flavours that certain fish are known to love…

Vanilla: A firm favourite for bream. You can get it in both liquid and powder form and as a specialised additive known as Brasem.

Curry powder: Roach love this, especially in winter. Also a good additive to maggots and one that other fish can fall for too, notably chub and barbel.

Fishmeal: Most species have become addicted to fishmeal and it is the central component of most of the pellets now used as feed and hook-bait by anglers.

Mollasses: This thick gooey liquid has always been noted as a bream attractant and helps bind together groundbait so you can form balls for throwing or catapulting. Any fish with a sweet tooth will be attracted, so expect a few carp and roach too.

Hemp: Ground up hempseed – or even the full, cooked grains – has always been a favourite bait for roach. But it is also loved by carp and is a great bait for holding many species in your swim.

The good and the bad

Would you eat the baits you use for fishing? Seriously!

If you were a fish would you munch on the maggots, worms, corn, bread, meat, boilies and pellets that you put on your own hook?

It's not such a mad question as you may think! Let's have a look at the poser…

How often have you opened your bait boxes and smelled that ammonia stench off maggots but still used them?

How often have you used worms that can barely offer a flicker of their tails as you put them on the hook?

How often have you put a boilie on a hair rig having taken great care to push a baiting needle through a bait that had obviously gone very hard and dried out far too much?

If there is anyone out there who can answer 'no' to the three questions above (or a similar one about any other bait) you are probably in a minority of one.

Yet you should *never* use any of the above baits if you are serious about catching fish.

Think human and fish at the same time. If someone gave you a stale bread sandwich you would have to be pretty hungry to eat it. If someone fed you a piece of meat (and basically that's what maggots are to fish) that smelt high you would reject it. So do something about it! Stinking baits are usually best thrown in the bin (when the other half isn't looking) but there are times when they can be 'rescued' or at least not wasted.

Maggots can be cleaned in sawdust, maize or even a bit of groundbait. Any of the above items will take away the sweat and they can then be riddled off. Any remaining smell can be got rid off with a few drops of flavouring – or even the smell of the groundbait you used to clean them up will help.

Dying worms are best ditched. You want ones that are moist and wriggly – like they had just come out of the ground or muck heap. If you are happy that they don't smell wrong you can still chop them up and use as feed.

Don't use casters that smell off. The late, great Ivan Marks once told me (and as usual the England international was right) that sour shells scare fish more than attract them. Bin them!

If the casters are floaters but haven't turned sour you can still use them on the hook. Roach in particular love a dark caster.

Stale bread – providing it isn't blue – can be steamed back to life, or whizz it around the microwave for a few seconds to get it back to a doughy texture. This is also a good ploy for slices to be used for bread punch. Crunchy stale bread can go into the liquidiser to make crumb groundbait that will just need a drop of water, as normal.

Rock hard boilies that still have some smell can be crushed for feed. There are crushers made specifically for this, or you can cut them up and smash them in a food processor (but not with a plastic holder, which can smash).

Left over fresh bait that isn't going to be used for some time can be frozen. Don't just stick maggots and casters in the fridge and hope they stay ok for a few weeks. Freeze them! Dead maggots are then fresh to feed or use on the hook. Fish, particularly bigger ones, love them. The casters should be placed straight into water when you defrost them or they will go grey and

Sitting and getting no bites? Maybe those sandwiches in your box will work!

be no use. I haven't tried freezing worms and can't see that really working. Live, fresh worms take some beating.

Pellets that have been soaked for feed or hook-baits can be frozen and used next time out. They are pretty hardy customers but don't freeze more than once – and only refreeze when they have been kept relatively cold during a fishing session.

Soaked pellets can get a bit soggy – or dry out – and will often need a flavour boost if they have been frozen.

Save cash and catch more fish in the process. But don't make false economies by risking the use of dodgy baits.

Completely different

Many anglers have often sat on the bank, looked at their sandwiches and thought: 'I wonder if I could catch with that on the hook?' Quite often they have pulled something out from between the bread slices, slipped it on their hook and landed a surprise specimen.

So here are a few baits that might appear a bit crazy, but which have all caught fish…

Baked beans: Yes, those in a can, complete with tomato sauce! Side hook or slip a few on a big hook or hair rig. Beans have always been a favourite with carp anglers.

Chips: Potatoes have caught in the past and a nice fried one is as appealing to fish as to you and me.

Orange peel: Cut into tiny tubes it has caught. Maybe it looks like sweetcorn or light pellets, the smell will certainly be attractive.

Specialist breads: Pitta and Nan breads can be used as floating baits and also offer a dough bait that is a bit tastier than your normal slices.

Chocolate bars: You have to be able to resist eating them yourself but various chocolate/toffee bars do catch. No surprise when chocolate powder is a key additive to some groundbaits.

Pasta: You can colour it, flavour it, cook it soft, hard or nice and chewy. Pasta also comes in various shapes and sizes giving you a very flexible bait.

Raisins: Really they are just a sweet particle. Soak well before use so that they slip on a hook or a hair.

Dog and cat biscuits: Pretty standard fare as floating baits for carp but check out the pet-food shelves for the more unusual flavours, shapes and coloured ones – being different can often score when regular baits have failed.

Catfood: Not so unusual, as it has been a popular choice for both carp and catfish anglers for a number of years. You can also use this to make up a paste by adding semolina. A few centuries ago chopped up cats and rabbits were used to make paste – this is definitely not recommended!

Instant desserts: These powders come in a variety of flavours and are usually mixed with milk to form a nice soft after-dinner dessert. Try adding them to your groundbait for extra flavour – or mix with breadcrumbs or semolina to form a paste hook bait.

How many baits?

How many different baits do you take with you when you go for a day's fishing?

One main bait and one change bait is probably normal for many pleasure anglers.

Carp anglers probably have a favourite flavour or make of boilie they stick with, whilst match anglers are more than likely to have a good selection of baits.

So how many do you really need? There's no finite number but there are definite guidelines that can boost your final bag of fish.

Take your favourite bait. It might sound obvious but confidence in the bait and tackle you use is a big thing in fishing. In my case this would usually be maggots or worms. There are few fish that will not eat these and even less days when they will not work. However, as the weather gets warmer these small natural baits can be a magnet for smaller fish and not let you get through to the bigger fish. Therefore meat and sweetcorn are my next two baits. Meat nearly always catches and when it doesn't corn usually will! Corn works all year not just summer. It's a bait that stays on your hook well for casting and you can use more than one grain on the right size hook.

Pellets and paste are next. There is no doubt that pellets are now a very important part of an angler's bait armoury but don't sit there like a dummy when they won't work. Try other baits – even different size and flavour pellets can sometimes catch when one variety doesn't raise as much as a sniff. Soft will often outscore hard pellets, even though they do come off the hook pretty easily at the attentions of small fish.

Paste isn't for everyone but there are now enough ready-made and good make-it-yourself mixes on the market to help you get a great hook-bait that stays on the hook. Paste will certainly deter those smaller fish and tends to be pretty instant once fish are in your swim. Ensure you fish it just on the bottom for best results.

Bread is a very important attractor and one overlooked on a lot of waters where it can work well. Paste, crust, flake, punch – a few slices gives you a big selection of alternatives.

If I had any two of the above baits I would be happy on the bank. Just one and I would be worried I could struggle. The more baits you carry the better your chances of catching, so long as you don't swap and change all of the time without giving the fish a chance to prove they fancy snacking on your bait.

A change could give you an edge, particularly on a well-fished water.

TIPS

- Rather than take a load of one hook-bait with you when you go fishing try taking a selection. There is nearly always one bait that works best on any one day – but fish do tend to wise up after they have been caught on a bait a few times.

- Don't stick rigidly to one bait on the hook. Double up maggots, worms, corn, pieces of meat, pellets... anything providing your hook is big enough. Sometimes that extra bit of grub makes the fish pounce.

- Bits of worms often outscore whole ones. A great trick is to cut a worm in two and put both on the hook, with the torn ends opposite each other. Or you can use a bit of worm the same size of a maggot to catch well – particularly roach, bream and carp in winter.

- Meat left exposed to the air will have skin formed on its surface that will make it easier to keep on the hook. But sometimes this skin will put choosy fish off taking your hook-bait.

- Mixed up groundbait can be kept for another day. If you are going to use it within 48 hours it should keep fine in a fridge. If you want to keep it for longer, seal it in a plastic bag and freeze. Defrost well before use as you may need to add extra water and riddle to get the right consistency.

- Don't add loads of particles to your groundbait after mixing. Just add the free offerings as you fill up a feeder or make up a ball of groundbait – that way you can judge exactly what extra food is going into your swim.

- On fast moving waters, mix groundbait wet and form firm balls to get it to the bottom. Try not to make them totally round, so they do not get pushed away by the flow. The addition of gravel or pebbles can help get groundbait down to the bottom fast in heavy flows.

- Soil is a great additive for groundbait. It binds the bait and makes it heavier. If you collect the soil from fresh molehills and riddle it the chances are that there are many little creatures and bugs in the mix that will also help attract fish.

Chapter 3

Species Guide

Barbel

British record: 21lb 1 oz (9.55 kg), Great Ouse.

Specimen size: 7lb (3.17 kg).

Venues: rivers, stillwaters.

Best baits: meat, spicey-flavoured baits, boilies, worms, big bunches of maggots or casters, sausages, luncheon meat.

FACT

Research has shown barbel are nomadic and will often swim great distances. Fish have been caught more than 20 miles away from what was regarded as their usual haunts.

Barbel are primarily a river fish, but in recent years they have been stocked into stillwaters also. Many barbel fishing purists have spoken out loudly about putting the species in lakes where they don't breed, but anglers who have caught these fish in stillwaters will point out that the species grows well and is in excellent condition, retaining all of its fighting qualities. Barbel are still more associated with fast flowing water and although they are known to like gravel bottoms where they search out food, they will also be found in deeper, slower water, especially in cooler weather.

Despite being more widespread in the UK than ever before, the barbel has become a sought-after quarry with a big fish still a very much-prized capture.

Over the past two decades barbel have increased in size dramatically, something which has been credited to them eating high protein based baits fed by anglers. Some smaller tributary rivers now hold many big barbel which appear to have sought the quiet sanctuary of these venues compared to major rivers where they once lived.

 TIPS

- **Barbel love cover, especially lots of flowing weed. You can often wear polarised sunglasses and watch barbel drift out from under weed to take food items in the clear water.**

- Pre-bait a number of likely looking swims and carefully make your way up and down the riverbank trying these areas for a short period at a time. At some point during the day a barbel may just take a fancy to one of these free food areas.

- Barbel are one of the strongest fighting fish around so don't be tempted to fish too light. It is one thing hooking them, another to get them into your net.

- Because they fight so hard barbel expend a lot of their energy when hooked. Every fish should be held gently in the water, its head pointing upstream, until it has recovered and can swim away strongly.

- Barbel should, whenever possible, not be retained in nets or tubes. They do not react well to captivity like this and their fins can be damaged.

Bream

British record: 22lb 11oz (10.29kg), Ferry Lagoon, Cambridgeshire.
Specimen size: 5lb-plus (2.27kg-plus).
Venues: rivers, lakes and canals.
Best baits: worms, maggots, casters, boilies.

FACT

In the middle of winter, when many stillwater fish prove hard to catch, bream can save the day! They are slower than many species and often do not get to baits fast enough in summer when carp are on the move. But in winter, when carp don't move around so much, the bream have a chance of getting to your bait.

Despite their lack of fighting qualities – all but the biggest of bream are not the greatest battlers – bream are a much-loved species. From bream under a couple of pounds (1kg) – often referred to as skimmers – to fish much bigger, they are a species that can offer a big challenge.

Bream can be finicky biters or very selective in what bait they will take. They often inhabit certain areas of rivers and lakes with a reluctance to move. But once you locate a shoal of bream and get them eating they can feed with abandon and a huge catch is on the cards. A shoal of bream – even a small one – can get through a vast quantity of bait. That's why many pleasure anglers like to locate where they live and then prebait the area with a lot of groundbait and particles such as sweetcorn and chopped up worms.

TIPS

- Bream like plenty of groundbait but it often doesn't pay to throw any into the water where they are already feeding – these fish don't like bait falling onto their heads or backs. Try to trickle in bait.

- Bream can change their feeding habits, even whilst you are catching them well. One minute you will be catching fish after fish on one bait; the next your swim will go totally quiet. A change to another hook-bait can bring instant rewards.

- After you have caught a few bream try casting a bit further out, to the side of where you were fishing, or even drop a cast short. Bigger fish often hang around on the edge of a shoal – but trying a slightly different spot to the main feed area will also mean less chance of spooking the fish.

Carp

British record: 67lb 8oz (30.62kg), Conningbrook, Kent.
Specimen size: 20lb (9.07kg).
Venues: stillwaters, rivers, canals.
Best baits: boilies, bread, bunches of dead maggots, worms.

FACT

Despite looking totally different, common, leather and mirror carp are all part of the same family.

Carp were once regarded as the most difficult fish to catch and were only targeted by a handful of very serious big fish anglers. But over the past few decades carp have become the No.1 species in the UK. They are the main fish in virtually every commercial fishery,

have their own range of baits and tackle and are now one of the first fish many newcomers to the sport will catch.

Carp will respond to almost all baits and every method, and even small specimens fight hard. Although a lot more 20lb-plus (9kg-plus) fish are now caught that is still the first target specimen weight for many anglers.

Carp do not live solely in stillwaters. Big fish can also be found in canals, particularly in and around wide areas like marinas. And a specimen river carp is regarded as a prime catch by many anglers, as these fish are often difficult to locate in flowing water.

TIPS

- A great way to catch carp is to get them feeding on the surface to baits like bread crust or dog biscuits. Throw in a few free offerings, wait until the fish are taking them readily and then get your bait carefully into the area.

- A controller float is used to cast light surface baits to carp. These can be overcast and then dragged carefully back into the feeding area.

- Carp love to prowl the margins and the biggest fish can often be caught right near the edge at the end of the day. If the water is around 18 inches (45cm) to 2 feet (60cm) deep, that is ideal depth.

Catfish

British record: 62lb (28kg), Withy Pool, Bedfordshire*.

Specimen size: 30lb (13.6kg).

Venues: selected stillwaters, some rivers.

Best baits: Live and dead fish, luncheon meat, bunches of worms, squid, liver.

* The catfish is no longer recognised for an official British record as it is not native. There have been a number of 100lb-plus (45kg-plus) specimens caught in the UK.

FACT

The catfish is non-native to the UK but has spread to a number of venues over the past couple of decades. On mainland Europe, particularly Spain, fish to 200lb-plus (90kg-plus) have been caught regularly on rod and line.

TIPS

- When possible, freeline your hook-baits. Cats can be very wary and will often play with baits before taking. At the first sign of any resistance from line or weights they can drop hook-baits.

- Because catfish have teeth like velcro pads that can easily wear through normal nylon line, use Dacron braid or specialist catfish hook lengths. For really big catfish, wire traces are used but should be avoided where possible.

- Cats have a great sense of smell – something worth remembering when selecting hook-baits. They are also often not fussy if bait is fresh or stinking!

- Night is best for catfish that are mostly nocturnal feeders. There are places they feed during the day, but shady areas and coloured water produce best results.

- Leeches are great baits as they are rarely, if ever, taken by other fish. But you will need to buy these and they can work out very expensive!

Chub

British record: 9lb 5oz (4.22kg), Southern Stillwater.

Specimen size: 5lb (2.27kg).

Venues: rivers, streams, lakes and canals.

Best baits: meat, cheese, maggots, casters, lobworms, bread, deadbaits.

FACT

Chub always used to be regarded as a river fish but some specimens in lakes and gravel pits have grown to record-breaking weights.

TIPS

- Cheese paste is one of the greatest chub baits. You can make it by soaking a few slices of bread and then mixing with grated cheese. Danish blue or any really pungent cheese is a great choice.

- Chub don't always pull your rod tip right round when legering. Sometimes it is best to wait until after the first short tap which is the fish checking out the bait.

- Never ignore any cover in the form of tree branches, rafts of rubbish or weed beds. Chub lay in wait for their prey fish under these obstacles.

- Chub favour clear water but you will catch them in flood conditions, often right next to the bank and with a nice big freshly collected lobworm.

- Dace and chub look pretty similar and when they are both small can easily be confused. The easy way to tell them apart is to check their caudal fin – the one at the back and lower side of the fish, before the tail. The chub's is convex (bends outwards) and the dace's is concave (curves inwards).

Crucian Carp

British record: 4lb 9oz* (1.93kg).
Specimen size: 1lb 8oz (0.68kg).
Venues: mainly stillwaters.
Best baits: maggots, worms, pellets, paste, bread.

* Three fish recorded at this size but record claims open at 4lb 8oz (2.04kg) for DNA tested fish.

FACT

True crucian carp are often confused with small common carp, brown goldfish and hybrids. They do hybridise with some other species so a true specimen is a sought-after fish.

Crucian are the smallest of the carp fishing family but a specimen-sized fish is still highly regarded by anglers. Noted as very shy biters, crucians will sometimes hardly move a float or a quivertip – but they fight exceptionally well for their size.

A true crucian has fantastic golden colours, similar to that of butter, which makes them a very attractive fish. Found in venues that range from farm ponds to be open waters, crucians will feed all day but can be tempted a lot easier at dawn and dusk. Weed and tree cover are good starting points and they often live right in the margins of venues too.

TIPS

- Small hooks and baits with light lines are the order of the day for most crucian carp fishing. Try fishing a light pole float rig on a rod and reel set up – and dot the float right down until it is just a pimple on the surface.

- Use a soft rod or soft elastic with your pole because, despite being shy biters, crucians can fight hard and will often swim away fast when first hooked. You don't want the hook to pull out against a stiff rod or heavy duty elastic.

- Paste is a great summer bait for crucian carp. This bait means you can also fish a bigger hook. Fish paste just on the bottom and strike if the float lifts or dips under.

Dace

British record: 1lb 5oz 2drm (595.34g), River Wear, Durham.

Specimen size: 8oz (226.80g).

Venues: rivers.

Best baits: maggots, casters.

FACT

Despite being a freshwater fish, dace have been found in brackish water near the sea. Dace can turn up in stillwaters but they are primarily a flowing venue species that love clean water conditions. They are found in small streams through to big rivers and although they don't grow big they offer an exciting challenge and can be caught in numbers, as they are often a shoal fish. They will live in very fast water or smooth glides, depending on the time of year and oxygen content in the venue.

Float fishing is by far the best option of catching this species that can be very fast biting.

TIPS

- Be ready to strike at any movement of the float when dace fishing. They have a habit of grabbing baits very fast and then letting go.

- Loose feeding maggots or casters are often the best idea for dace but sometimes they do respond well to regular offerings of groundbait.

- Dace, roach and chub can often be found in the same areas of a river.

- Fly anglers often catch dace by accident whilst trout fishing – proving that this is a great species to catch on that method.

Eel

British record: 11lb 2oz (5.04kg), Kingfisher Lake, Hampshire.

Specimen size: 4lb (1.81kg).

Venues: most waters.

Best baits: worms, deadbaits.

FACT

European eels travel thousands of miles to spawn, visiting the Sargasso Sea in the Atlantic Ocean near Bermuda. Eels are nowhere near as prolific as they were a decade ago and great care should be taken to protect stocks.

Many anglers do not like catching eels because of their slimy bodies and the fact they can cause massive tangles in end rigs. But a big eel is a crafty creature to fool and a determined fighter that will test tackle to the utmost.

There has been a big decrease in the number of eels in recent years that has led to bans on fishing for them in some places. They are a protected species that means any taken on rod and line must be returned to the water.

- Unhooking eels can be a tricky process, but if you lay them on their backs in a small groove made in earth they often lay still.

- The biggest eels tend to be caught from unpressured venues and in warmer weather.

- Large eels are often found in venues that have very steep banks – the theory being that the eels get into the water and then cannot climb out, where they would normally make their way across wetland to reach rivers before migrating to the sea to spawn.

Gudgeon

British record: 5oz (142g), River Nadder, Wiltshire.

Specimen size: 2oz (57g).

Venues: rivers, stillwaters, canals.

Best baits: maggot.

FACT

Gudgeon are referred to by a number of nicknames, including Gobies (after their latin name of Gobio gobio) and Pongos (usually a bigger gudgeon). It's not the biggest coarse fish around but many anglers love the humble gudgeon.

Gudgeon are a hardy, attractive species that live in shoals. That means you can often catch quite a few of them at a time – and they will often feed in even the worst weather and both in low and flood conditions.

TIPS

- Gudgeon will take big maggots but are also quite partial to smaller pinkie maggots.

- Groundbait is an effective way to lure gudgeon into your swim. Don't put many hook baits into the groundbait.

- Don't confuse a gudgeon with a small barbel just because they both have barbules. A gudgeon has two of these that are used to detect food, a barbel has four.

Perch

British record: 6lb 3oz (2.8kg) (2), Stream Valley Lakes, East Sussex, Wilstone Reservoir, Hertfordshire.
Specimen size: 2lb 8oz (1.13kg).
Venues: rivers, lakes and canals.
Best baits: worms, maggots, casters, small fish and even prawns.

FACT

The sharp fins on the back of a perch are *not* poisonous! But they can inflict some serious cuts on your fingers, so these fish should be handled with care.

There are few better sights than a big perch with its giant mouth, big spikey fins and lovely colourings. A small perch is often the first fish that newcomers land; a bigger specimen is a lot harder to attempt.

Many venues hold perch, as they are one of the most widespread species in Europe, living in anything from weeded-up canals to big Scottish lochs. But only a handful of waters hold numbers of big perch – and you will usually find these in venues that have not had a lot of pressure from anglers in the past few years. Canals and commercial fisheries have seen a boom in big perch over recent years.

Perch do not like bright light conditions. Dull, overcast days are best for catching specimens that often live next to structures like platforms, bridges, overhanging trees and moored boats. They hover quietly in these places as they wait for smaller fish to swim past so they can intercept and eat them.

TIPS

- Perch have hard mouths. That means sharp hooks are a must to get a good hold, and these fish should not be played too hard or the hook could pull out.

- Perch, even big ones, are often pack fish. If you land one there is a good chance there are a few more around and ready to feed.

- Smaller perch also tend to shoal up which means once you start catching them you may have trouble getting your bait to a bigger one!

- You can often spot where perch are feeding by watching for fry fish leap out of the water as they are chased before being eaten!

- Big perch tend to show in cycles. They often show for a few years and then all but disappear only to return out of the blue.

Pike

British record: 46lb 13oz (21.23kg), Llandegfedd Reservoir, Wales.

Specimen size: 20lb (9.07kg).

Venues: rivers, reservoirs, lakes and canals.

Best baits: live and dead fish, artificial lures and spinners.

FACT

Former Wales rugby star Gareth Edwards set a new British best for pike when he landed a 45lb 6oz (20.58kg) specimen from Llandegfedd Reservoir in 1990. It was a record for two years.

The pike is a torpedo-shaped predator, an efficient killing machine that takes no prisoners when it is in a feeding mood. Even small pike look mean but impressive. A big pike is something that all anglers can admire for its shape, power and often-pronounced markings that are its camouflage when it lurks near weed-beds awaiting its prey.

Small pike are fairly easy to catch, especially when using spinners. But their larger brothers have to be tracked down and then carefully fooled. Although the biggest pike tend to be found in large venues like Scottish lochs and trout fishing reservoirs, there are a number of lakes that hold big fish. You will also find specimen pike in canals and rivers. A big river pike is something that many anglers rate very highly.

TIPS

- Try colouring deadbaits so they stand out from other fish, or increase their attraction by injecting fish oils. These oils create a scent trail in the water that the pike can home in on.

- Strike firmly but quickly after a pike takes your bait to avoid deep hooking.

- If possible, go on an organised course to learn how to fish for and unhook pike. A deeply hooked pike needs special care but hooks can be removed safely. This is a tricky job but once you are shown how to do the task it is fairly easy.

- Wherever possible, use barbless hooks for pike to make unhooking easier and so there is less damage to this delicate fish. If you use trebles just one of the hooks could be semi-barbed so it holds your bait more efficiently.

- Pike will feed in most weather conditions but winter is when the species is at its best in terms of weight and fighting ability.

- Never stand up when having your picture taken with a pike, or a carp. Kneel and keep the fish close to the ground over a good unhooking mat so that should it flip out of your grasp it doesn't get damaged.

- Never leave your pike baits cast into the water and rods unattended. The pike could be gut hooked and that could be fatal to the fish.

Roach

British record: 4lb 4oz (1.93kg), Northern Ireland*.

Specimen size: 2lb (0.91kg).

Venues: everywhere.

Best baits: bread, casters, worms, hemp seed, tares sweetcorn, mini boilies.

* Open for DNA claims at 3lb 12 oz (1.70kg).

FACT

Dusk is the prime time to catch a big roach. Just as the light begins to fade you will see them roll and specimens appear to become less wary and more ready to take a hook-bait. Carp may be the most sought-after fish in the UK but roach can probably still be classed as the most popular.

Big roach or big nets of prime specimens are a prized catch among many leading anglers. Ask many anglers which they would rather have, a 100 lb (45kg) net of carp or a 20 lb (9kg) net of roach, and the smaller catch of redfins would probably win!

Catching a big roach or a net of them takes skill but the achievement is one that is recognised by all experienced anglers. Small roach can be easy to catch but bigger fish are not so common and can also be very wary. Tackle and bait have to be spot-on. Presentation and feeding also need to be precise, although there will be the odd red-letter day when the roach feed like crazy!

Roach are happy in stillwaters, rivers and canals. They also tend to feed better when conditions are not so bright, and when there is coloured water.

- Fish as light as possible. Roach can quickly suss out thick line and big hooks.

- Roach have a sweet tooth so try using sweeteners to boost your hook-baits and groundbait.

- Roach, rudd and hybrids of roach and bream can easily be confused. A true roach's top lip protrudes over the bottom one and there are between 10 and 14 rays on its anal fin. There are more rays on a hybrid.

- Cooked hemp seed can be great bait for roach. Feed little and often but don't fish over the top of this straight way. Let the fish have plenty of time to get confident in eating the bait. Some anglers feed for two hours or more before giving the feed area a try. Fish a single grain on the hook or try a bigger tare.

- Roach move around quite a lot so expect them to change their haunts in both lakes and rivers during the course of a season and at different times of the year.

- The last hour of light and the first few hours of darkness are the top times for catching good roach.

Rudd

British record: 4lb 10oz (2.08kg) (2) both from Armagh*.
Specimen size: 1lb 8oz (0.68kg).
Venues: mostly stillwaters, some canals and rivers.
Best baits: maggots, casters, bread, sweetcorn, worms.

* Open for DNA claims over 3lb 12oz (1.7kg).

FACT

Rudd often appear in venues in vast shoals, and then disappear again just as quickly! This is probably down to their life cycles and breeding habits.

Many beginners confuse the rudd with roach because their colours can be very similar. Both species have orange-red fins, are a similar shape and sometimes even have the same silvery scales. But a true rudd sticks out from a true roach like a sore thumb. The rudd will have a protruding bottom lip because it is more of a surface feeder and its body colours will be almost golden rather than silver. It can be very difficult to tell small roach and rudd apart but as they get bigger the difference does become more apparent.

The water the fish live in does have an effect on their colours and can lead to confusion. Rudd like clear water and this is where their true more golden body colour will show more.

TIPS

- Bigger rudd live near weeds, lily pads and rushes where they are more likely to take hook-baits.

- Rudd often tend to feed off the bottom and even on the surface. They can be targeted with floating baits such as a piece of bread.

- If you catch a big rudd there's every chance there are another one or two nearby so don't move straight away.

Tench

British record: 15lb 3oz 6drm (6.88kg), Sheepwalk Pit, Surrey.
Specimen size: 5lb (2.26kg)
Venues: lakes, ponds, canals.
Best baits: worms, bread, casters, maggots, boilies, paste.

FACT

Although primarily a fish that lives in stillwaters and canals, tench can be caught in some slower moving rivers.

There is no mistaking a tench for another species – its body shape, small red eyes and tiny scales give the fish a distinct identity. Although often referred to as olive green in colour, tench can also appear almost black through to nearly yellow. Their body colour is often a reflection on the water in which they are present, the more usual green tench coming from fairly clear waters. Dark bottomed lakes tend to produce darker tench whilst coloured venues yield lighter coloured fish. Some fish breeders have also produced other colours of the species.

Tench often feed best early and late in the day but in venues where the water is coloured they will take baits all day, even when the sun is bright.

Their big fins and powerful tails ensure they can fight well and many times it will feel like you have hooked a much bigger fish than is actually on the end of your line.

TIPS

- Tench love to feed early morning and will often giveaway their presence as they grub around the bottom mud looking for food and release tiny air bubbles.

- Pre-baiting is a good move for tench. It can get the fish feeding in an area and they can be waiting there when you start to fish.

- Primarily a bottom feeding fish, like most species tench will come up in the water to take baits. Steady feeding can see the tech rise right off the bottom.

- Keep an eye on rushes and lily pads whilst tench fishing – the fish will often brush against them and make them shake. But remember the movement could be carp or other big fish!

Zander

British record: 21lb 5oz (9.67kg), River Severn.

Specimen size: 10lb (4.54kg).

Venues: lakes, canals, rivers.

Best baits: small coarse fish deadbaits, lures.

FACT

The zander, sometimes known as the pike-perch, is not a hybrid of the two species but is related to the perch family.

Originally introduced to the Fenland area of England, zander have now spread to a number of river systems, including the Trent, Severn and Thames. They also live in a number of canals in the Midlands and in some lakes around the country. They are not noted for their fighting qualities but are still a popular quarry for many predator anglers. They are present in many mainland European waters but not in Ireland.

Zander are another species that prefer darker conditions and are often nocturnal feeders, or feed better in floods.

TIPS

- Sea and freshwater fish deadbaits score best for the zander, although it will take spinners and lures.

- Coloured water or night are the best conditions for zander which have vision that is far superior to other predators such as pike.

- You will need to use a wire trace to combat the species' sharp teeth but must also remember that zander are very suspicious of any weight or resistance and may easily drop baits.

- Strike quickly at any signs of a bite as zander quite often swallow baits quickly which can lead to deep hooking.

Other UK record fish

These are a mix of mini-species records, the more unusual and lesser distributed UK fish, and some species which are either not really fished for on rod and line or are now no longer accepted for records.

The records here are ones ratified by the British Record (rod-caught) Fish Committee. Many specialist angling organisations, which often promote individual species, have their own record lists.

Bitterling
12drm (21g), Barway Lake, Cambridgeshire.

Bleak
4oz 9drm (129g) River Lark, Cambridgeshire.

Brown goldfish
5lb 11oz 8drm (2.594kg), stillwater, Surrey.

Bullhead
1oz (28.35g), Green River, Surrey.

Catfish (Bullhead, black)
1lb 3oz 1drm (540.41g) Lake Meadows, Essex.

Golden orfe
8lb 5oz (3.77kg) Lymm Vale, Cheshire.

Grass carp
44lb 8oz (20.18kg), Horton Church Lake, Berks.

Minnow
13.5oz (382.72g), Whitworth Lake, County Durham.

Pumpkinseed
14oz 2drm (400.44g), Tanyard Fishery, Sussex.

Ruffe
5oz 4drm (148.83g), West View Farm, Cumbria.

Schelly (Skelly)
2lb 1oz 9drm (951.48g), Haweswater Reservoir, Cumbria.

Silver Bream
3lb 4oz (1.47kg), Mill Farm, Sussex.

Stickleback (3-spined)
4drm (7g), High Flyer Lake, Ely, Cambridgeshire.

Stone Loach
13drm (23g), Windmill Fishery, Bristol.

Walleye
11lb 12oz (5.33kg), River Delph, Norfolk.

Chapter 4

Floats and Legers

4.1 Floats

Floats have two primary aims in fishing – to give you casting weight and to act as a bite detector.

Although there are hundreds of different types of floats, they can be split into three simple categories: bottom end only, top and bottom, pole.

Bottom end only floats are better known as wagglers. They attach to your line only at their bottom end via a ring or an adaptor. They can be used on rivers and stillwaters and are best for distance fishing.

Top and bottom floats are attached to your line with the use of silicone sleeves at the top and bottom of the floats and are better known as stick floats or balsas. They are more associated with running water fishing.

No surprise that pole floats are made primarily for fishing with a pole – although nowadays a lot of anglers will also use a pole float with rod and reel for fishing down the edge on stillwaters.

All three styles of float come in a myriad of patterns, weights, lengths, sizes, colours and are constructed from a whole variety of materials, including bird quills, various grade balsa woods and polystyrene foam.

It would take a whole book to describe every pattern and model in detail so this is only meant as a general guide to what to use and when. You will also discover your own favourite patterns and makes of float, or may even start to make your own, to cover the various fishing challenges you face.

Wagglers (left to right): Straight, insert, short and thin topped dart for caster for canal fishing.

Wagglers

There are two basic types of waggler: straight and bodied. For most fishing, straight wagglers – often made from peacock quills – will suffice. Bodied wagglers, that have a bulbous body at the base, are mainly for greater distance, rough conditions or when these floats are being used as slider floats.

Wagglers can have thinner insert tips, to be used when bites are shy. They can also have fatter bodies for their whole lengths, usually for river fishing when dragging a few shot along the bottom. The current does not drag under the thicker tips easily. Both versions are also available with loaded bases so that you do not have to put as much shot on your line to dot the float down to its tip. Some of these loadings are adjustable, often by adding or removing weights or rings.

When fishing a waggler, the bulk of the shot needed to cock the float – anything up to three quarters of its capacity – should be around the base of the float. This helps prevents tangles but more important lets you cast much easier.

Crystal or clear wagglers are made from plastic which many anglers believe does not cast the same

Basic pole float shapes (left to right): Bodied for carrying larger weights, body up for river, all-round rugby-ball type shape, body down for stillwater.

Crystal wagglers, loaded (top) and bodied.

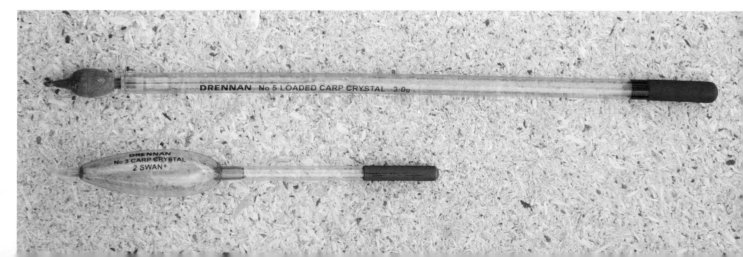

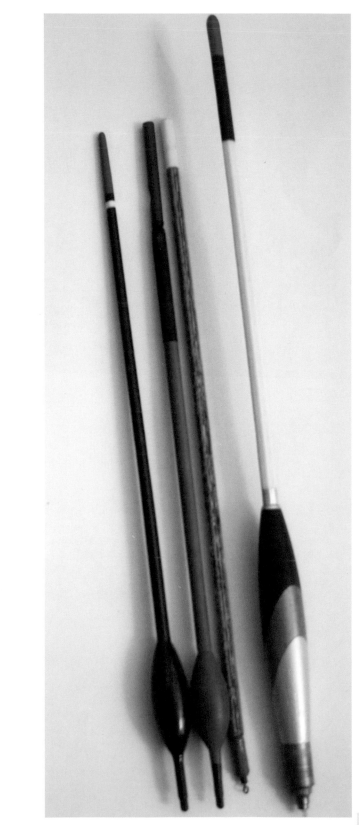

Bodied and loaded wagglers.

shadow as normal floats – and so therefore does not spook fish so easily. Crystals are a great alternative in clear water, when fishing shallow or when there is little depth.

Sticks and Balsas

By using a float fastened top and bottom to your line you can have great control over your tackle and dictate how your bait performs in the water. You can hold the float back against the flow to make the bait lift enticingly; let it go with the current; guide the bait through nice runs; or even hold it steady in a piece of slack water. Although primarily a method for fishing at close range, a heavier top and bottom float cast carefully can be fished at bigger distances.

Balsa floats are much more buoyant so carry much greater weights or shot, which make them excellent for faster and more turbulent water. Many anglers use these with big baits – like bread and meat – with a big bulk of shot down the line and then just one or two large dropper shot between this and the hook. The aim

Adjustable ring weights at based of a loaded waggler.

Hollow tips on a waggler mean you still have a sensitive float that can be seen at distance.

here is to get the bait down but still retain control over your gear.

Stick floats, although they can be fished with a bulk and then droppers, are often fished shirt button style – with the shot spaced along the line. It is often best to put the majority of the shot half way or lower down your line between the bottom of the float and the hook, depending on the depth you are fishing. This will reduce tangles.

Always feather your line after casting a float – that is to say slow it down gently by trapping the line with your finger against the spool of the reel when you get to the required distance – so that the hook goes into the water first, ahead of the shot and the float. This will prevent tangles and means you are also fishing and ready to register a bite as soon as your bait is in the water.

Top and bottom floats (left to right): Balsa, wire-stemmed stick, cane stemmed stick, dome topped stick.

Stick variations

Even stick floats come in a variety of patterns. The main ones are:

Balsa and cane: A balsa body and cane stem. Used for fishing your bait on the drop, mid-depth, holding back or running through in water up to 2.4 metres (8 feet) deep. Conditions need to be near-perfect with little wind. Use a pointed top when there is no wind, a domed top when conditions are a bit rougher.

Heavy: Balsa bodies but with a heavier base, such as lignum, which makes them a bit easier to cast and control. Used in water from 1.8 to 3.6 metres (6 to 12 feet) deep and when there is a bit more flow and you want to hold back the bait.

Alloy or wire: Usually a balsa body, although it can be other materials, such as polystyrene, with a wire, aluminium or similar heavy stem which gives them great stability in faster water. They are not so easy to cast.

Plastic: The purists would wince at the thought of a stickfloat with a plastic base – and with good reason as they do not offer the same control as traditional materials. But there are versions with clear plastic bases that many anglers believe offer the same advantage as clear wagglers.

Pole

Pole floats used to be balsa bodies, wire stems and plastic bristles to give sensitive bite indication. Now there are lots of different patterns for various conditions, depths and species. Again, we will split patterns down into simple format. Most have balsa or a type of foam for their bodies. An oval-shaped body, a bit like a rugby ball, is the best all round pattern for both still and running waters. But you will also get body up floats – similar in shape to a pear with the thickest part at the top – which are best for moving water. Body down floats – the pear shape with the fat bit at the bottom – are good for stability in stillwaters.

Some pole floats have slim bodies, which are great for fishing in stationary or slow moving water when fish are shy, or for fishing baits that drop slowly through the water, like bread punch and maggots.

Tips can be made of wire (really sensitive and difficult to shot correctly), plastic bristle (the most common for good bite indication), cane (for big baits) or can be hollow plastic – which give good bite indication with a fair bit of the tip still showing and can more easily be seen at distance.

Stems can be made of plastic (often for fishing on the drop), wire (for stability) or cane (fishing to hand).

These are only very general guidelines but can be used to try and match up the float to the type of venue you fish.

There are also specialist floats, many for commercial carp fisheries, with reinforced side eyes just under the bristle.

Various dibber floats, used to float fish in shallow water or near the surface.

The term dibber is often used to describe a very short pole float, sometimes with a domed top, that is used to fish down the edge, either at close range or distance, maybe against a far bank of a canal of narrow lake, and in shallow water.

TIPS

- Always use a big enough float to cast the distance you want with ease. If you really have to thrash your rod to get the distance, your float is too light and needs to be able to carry more weight.

- You can place a piece of coloured silicone tubing – the stuff you normally use on stick floats – over the tip of your waggler or stick to change its colour.

- Even if there is an inch of colour painted onto the top of your float, always shot it down as far as possible, certainly with no more than 90mm (3/8 inch) showing.

- To slow your bait's passage through your swim when fishing a river you can leave a good bit of the float showing and let a few small shot drag along the bottom. The more buoyant tip will not pull under every time the shot hits a small obstacle.

- Don't be afraid to change your shotting pattern whilst fishing if you stop getting bites. Fish may have come up or gone down in the water chasing food – or a warmer air temperature might have seen them come nearer the surface. A slight movement of a few shot to alter the fall of your bait through the water can make a massive difference.

- Match your float to the depth of water you are fishing. A short dibber is great for shallow water no more than 46cm (18 inches) deep but you might want a waggler that could be 46cm (18 inches) long to fish water more than 2.5 metres (8 feet) deep.

- A back shot can help you present a bait even better in running or stillwater. This is a shot you place just above the float – or a couple of feet above it. In rivers this can help you control the float better and keep it in a straight line. On stillwaters, when pole fishing, this shot will help prevent wind blowing the line, and then the

Stotz are a good alternative to shot, especially for light pole rigs or fishing a slow falling bait.

float, out of position, or aid in keeping it still. Back shot can be anything from a No.8 to an SSG, depending on what you need.

- Don't be frightened to over-shot your float so that it sinks in running water. This means you have to hold the float back hard to keep it just above water – but that will aid you in slowing down the bait.

- Always put three pieces of silicone rubber on a top and bottom float. These are to hold your line on the float and the top one should be just below the tip. The lowest should be at the base of the float and just stick over the end by a few millimetres ($1/10$ inch) to help prevent tangling. The third, placed about half way down, should be the right size so that you can push it up or down should one of your other rubbers break.

Shotting patterns

Shotting patterns are something that many inexperienced anglers get confused about. Some even believe that there is a holy grail of shotting patterns, one that catches more than any other. But quite simply there are just two basic patterns – strung out or bulk down with a dropper. Strung out shot is when the fish are willing to take bait on the drop, and is probably linked to warmer water fishing more than anything else. Bulk shotting is to get the bait down fast to the deck where the fish are feeding – or to get through the smaller fish that might be higher up in the water. Start with those two and adapt them to suit the conditions and species you are trying to catch and you won't go far

Place three silicone sleeves on a top and bottom float.

wrong. But in both cases you should always consider other possibilities; size of the shot on the line can be varied and where you place them should also be experimented with. Even during a fishing session if you are not getting bites or the fish appear to have gone off the feed try altering where the shot are on your line.

Good anglers experiment and rarely stick to one pattern or even fishing at one depth of water. It's not unusual for them to tweak shotting every 20 minutes if they are not catching or think they can catch faster. The shot are not there just to cock your float. They are there to help register bites and aid bait presentation. The flow of the water – even in lakes – the depth, wind and where the fish are feeding must all be taken into account when you shot up.

TIPS

- Try to avoid putting shot on your hook length. Clamping them on line can cause weak spots.

- Always get one shot as close to the hook as possible – even within 2-3cm (an inch or two). This is the tell-tale that registers the bites; your final guide that the rig has settled correctly in the water.

- If your float is shotted right but then doesn't cock as quickly as it should, strike. A fish has probably intercepted the bait on the way down and held up the shot.

- Count how long it takes each shot to take the float down to the level you set for cocking. Any variation in the time means a fish has the bait in its mouth.

- Use a number of small shot in groups when possible, rather than one big shot. These smaller shot – say No.8 or 9s – will give you a much better presentation and will cast better. They also give you more flexibility in changing from a bulk shot with droppers to strung out shot, without changing your rig during a session.

- Sometimes a bunch of big shot is useful for pulling a float through with the current, especially if there is a strong upstream wind.

- In rough conditions get as much weight on your line as possible to improve presentation.

- Play around with small shot to dot your float down so the smallest possible bit of it shows. You will be amazed at how many bites you never normally see... a pin head of float showing can register a bite you never knew you had when the float was even just a quarter of an inch out of the water.

- Stotz – very similar to Styl weights – are great for use on bigger diameter lines, as they don't ping off as easily as normal split shot. These tube-shaped weights are also good for stringing out as they fall slower through the water, giving bait a much more natural drop. They can also be removed easily.

4.2 Legering

Legering for many anglers is a case of tying on a weight and hook and then just casting into a lake or river. But for the more experienced angler this is a devastating method that, with a little thought, can bring big rewards. Fishing a leger or a swimfeeder correctly is as skilful as fishing with a float – and that is why there is now a World Championships for feeder fishing!

For lake fishing you need a big enough weight on your line to cast to the required distance and then tighten up your line quickly to the quivertip. A swimfeeder should carry enough bait to attract and hold fish in your swim, but not be so big that the splash scares away every fish in sight.

On a river you want a leger or swimfeeder that will hold bottom in the spot you have chosen to fish, with the feeder once again carrying enough bait to attract fish and hold them in that spot. But there are also many other things you need to think about when fishing baits in these ways. Some of the things you should be looking at are highlighted in the tips below.

Feeding basics

When you fish a leger or feeder you must also remember to keep feeding! It is so easy to just cast out and wait for the tip to pull round or drop back, but that might not happen if you don't offer the fish enough free offerings.

When you are legering remember to feed by hand or catapult every few minutes, or as bites dictate. More bites probably mean more fish, but if there are no bites still keep drip-feeding bait to attract fish. When you are using a swimfeeder it is easy to get your bait next to your hook. But that is no good in still or flowing water if you only cast every now and then. If you are catching fish every cast in it's easy to remember… as you fill the feeder on every cast.

Try to time yourself when to reel in and fill the feeder, even if you are not getting bites. Maybe give it five or ten minutes between casts.

It also pays to have a cast with just a leger on your line when you first start to fish to check if there are snags in your swim and to check the depth. Once you have decided where you want to fish fill the feeder and cast out five or six times to get some bait into the water and set a trap for the fish.

Casting

Two things are crucial to your fishing when fishing a leger or swimfeeder – especially on big rivers or large stillwaters.

1. Distance: Find where you want to fish, whether it is because of the depth or to a fish-holding feature. Do a few trial casts and once you get it right clip up your line. Many reels have line clips. If yours doesn't have one, or you are not happy with clipping up because of fear of a snap off on the cast or a good fish going on a big run, use a rubber band around your spool. Just in case you snag up or snap off make sure you know how far you have cast. You can do this by casting out and then counting how many turns of the reel handle

Line clip on fixed spool reel

it takes to retrieve your end rig. If you want to be doubly sure of the distance, put two bank sticks into the ground a good way apart and then once you have found your distance walk the line around the sticks to measure it. This way you can always tackle up again and have the same length of line out from your reel.

2. Accuracy: There's no point casting to the same distance every time if your bait isn't landing in the same place. What might look like the same spot to you could be metres apart at distance or on featureless venues. When you cast bring your rod straight over the top of your head and aim for a marker on the far bank, such as a tree or a fence post. Try to make sure that the length of line from your leger or feeder to the top of the rod is the same every time you cast, and don't reel the rig to the top ring on the rod – you will get tangled and get no distance to your cast. Also, do not have a big length of line from the tip to the rig or you will lose accuracy. The optimum length is usually around two to three feet, but you will best judge this for your own comfort in casting and also dictated to you by any tree branches that may be overhead.

TIPS

- On a stillwater you want an angle of at least 45 degrees from your quivertip to the feeder or leger so that you can see bites. Put a slight bend in the tip by tightening your line, then bites will either be a drop-back of the tip or the more usual pull round.

Keep your eyes on a far bank marker as you cast overhead.

Use a target board to help you see shy bites on your quivertip.

- On a flowing river you want just enough weight on the line so that you can hold bottom. Keep your rod high so as much line as possible is out of the flow; feed a bit of line off your reel to put a bow in the line but keep a bend in your quivertip. More often than not the rod will bounce back as the fish picks up the bait, moves the feeder or leger and hooks itself. You may still get pull rounds as bites too.

- They may look a bit old fashioned to many anglers who are used to carp tearing off with legered baits, but for more finicky feeders indicator boards are a great asset in spotting bites. Indicator or target boards – basically plastic boards with lines drawn on them – let you line up your tip with one of the lines and spot more easily, even a short movement on the tip.

- Most of the time you will have your line tight to your tip, but there are occasions when slack lining works. Cast out, tighten up and then – providing the flow allows, and usually in stillwaters – let out a short bit of line so that it is slack from the tip to the water. When fish are

really shy the bites will be shown by that slack starting to tighten.

- Always put your bait on the hook before filling your feeder with bait. If you put live bait like maggots in the feeder first, some of them will wriggle out before you bait the hook. If you are using a groundbait feeder it could slip into the water as you bait the hook and all of the feed will be washed out.

- When casting long distances, it can pay to tape over some of the holes on a maggot feeder – this stops the grubs being forced out on the cast.

- You can also tape over the holes if the bait comes out too fast on a fast flowing river, or if you want the maggots or groundbait to trickle out slowly in winter.

Rigs and traces

There are two basic rigs for legering – fixed or free running. Many venues, particularly commercial fisheries, insist on free running rigs. This is to ensure that if your line snaps a fish is not left dragging a rig around or, worse, drags the rig into a snag and become tethered. Fixed rigs are most suitable for open water fishing or when targeting fish that are not so powerful. If you do use a fixed rig ensure that you have a weaker trace or use an attachment that will allow the leger or feeder to come off the line should it snag.

On both rigs the length of your trace is a vital element to consider. Just like float fishing when you change the depth at which you fish, your trace length for legering should be varied during fishing until you find the best length. A long trace will allow a bait to fall slowly through the water, which is good for when fish are not feeding on the bottom or you want to explore a lot of your swim. When fish are also feeding shyly a longer trace will give them more confidence when they pick up the bait as they will be able to swim off without feeling resistance from a leger, feeder or your quivertip straight away.

A shorter trace will get your bait nearer your feed when using a swimfeeder and will also register bites faster. Fish can often give a quick indication on a short trace and then drop the bait resulting in missed bites. On a self-hooking or fixed rig a short trace usually works more efficiently.

A good starting point for a trace length is around two to three feet. Do not be worried about going as short as a 5cm (or a few inches) for method feeder fishing – or even as long as 1.5–2 metres (5–7 feet) for fishing on the drop.

Braid or line?

Many anglers are still split about which is best on the reel for fishing on the bottom – braid or normal nylon line. The general consensus of opinion is that for shy biting fish at distance braid is best. There is no stretch in braid so that when a fish picks up the bait even the smallest movement registers almost instantly on your quivertip. But for bigger fish, especially on lighter gear, nylon is better as it offers more stretch to guard against the lunges of specimens.

Anglers who fish braid on their reels often fish a shock leader of heavy line. This is tied to the end rig and to the braid on your reel and should go through the complete length of the rod and put a couple of turns on the reel spool too. Braid is a lot thinner than line in comparable breaking strains but for bottom fishing you must ensure that you buy a sinking braid or it will become very, very difficult to tighten your line to register a bite.

Fishing braid also requires the use of a leger rod that has a very soft, forgiving action. A fish can easily pull off the hook as the braid has no stretch and you need the cushioning action of the shock absorber and the rod to guard against this. Also, there is little need to strike hard when fishing braid; a gentle lift of the rod is usually enough to pull the hook home. Unlike line you are not also pulling against a stretch factor. The bonus of braid, as well as showing shy bites, is that you can really feel the fight of the fish through your rod.

Which feeder?

There are three basic patterns of feeder: open-end, block-end and method. You will see other swimfeeders for sale but they are basically more specialised versions of the above three. All of these models can be used on flowing or stillwaters, depending on conditions, the species you are after and what bait you want to feed.

Open-end versions are usually called groundbait feeders. As the name implies, there are no caps on this model. They are filled with your groundbait, often containing hook-bait samples. These feeders come in plastic tube versions, which are standard, but you can also get them in wire or plastic mesh that are called cage feeders. Cages will empty their bait faster and are great for shallow water or very little flow. Normal plastic feeders get bait to the bottom better.

Block-end feeders are often referred to as maggot feeders because that is their prime use. They are usually sealed at one end with a cap that opens on the other. Maggots – sometimes casters, chopped worms or small pellets – are put inside and then cast out. You will find tube shaped block-ends, some that are rectangular and models that carry weights on their side or at their ends. End weights cast better, side weights will hold the bottom more efficiently. Sometimes anglers block one end with groundbait, drop a load of bait in the middle and then create a sandwich by blocking the other end with more groundbait.

Method feeders were developed for fishing baits very close to the feeders – a system called the 'Method'! This was originally an idea for catching carp but has since proved useful in attracting a number of species. Basically, the Method involves shaping sticky groundbait or softened pellets around the feeder.

When firing a groundbait catapult keep your arm outstretched and pull the elastic back the same distance every time to ensure you hit the right spot.

Inset: Make sure all your balls of groundbait are the same size for catapulting.

The hook-bait is fished on a very short trace, often as little as 10cm (4 inches), and more often than not this is buried into the groundbait. As this feeder has a flattened base to which is attached its main weight, it always lands with the groundbait pile on top. Fish attack the mound of feed, find the hook-bait and dash off with it, often hooking themselves.

Do not strike at any indication on the rod tip. The initial taps and knocks are fish knocking the groundbait so they can eat it – and when they find the hook-bait they will take off like trains!

Swimfeeders (left to right): Flat Method, Plastic open-end, Cage/mesh, Block-end/maggot.

- Just because you are fishing a bait static on the bottom doesn't mean you have to sit motionless on your seat waiting for a bite. Sometimes a slight movement of the bait can make a fish pounce. Just twitch the bait slightly by lifting your rod or pulling a bit on your line.

- Try to fish and feed more than one area of your swim. Just giving one area a rest can bring it back to life. And fishing two areas in one swim is always a good bet to help you catch a few more fish.

- When you are fishing a leger or feeder try to imagine that you are fishing a float or pole – and that should help you to remember to keep feeding on a regular basis.

- Sometimes fish back off bait and will move to the side or further out from the area you have been feeding. Every so often, especially when you are not getting bites, try to cast to these areas and you will be surprised at how many bonus fish you get.

- Don't always rely on a feeder to get bait near your hook. Sometimes a straight leger fished with loose feed or balls of groundbait fed with a catapult can work better. But you must learn how to be accurate. Practice by firing balls of bait into a bucket in your garden or a field.

- When fishing the Method it pays to experiment with groundbait that will stay in a ball and some that will break up. Fish that have become wise to the hard ball that they attack will often respond better if the groundbait breaks down faster. Your hook-bait is still among the main feed, which makes it stand out.

- Although you want to be feeding in a pretty tight area remember that you can't catch a 50kg (100 lb) net of fish from a spot the size of a bucket! Spread the feed out a little bit, maybe the size of a small car's roof.

- When you are fishing a river the bait that goes out in the feeder or loose wont stay in the area you are fishing – it will get washed downstream. But this will help pull fish into your swim, providing you keep that trickle of bait going into the water.

- Modifying feeders is sometimes necessary so that they perform better. Do not be afraid to add weight so that they cast further or hold the bottom better; you can buy special add-on weights. Also, if bait does not come out of the feeder fast enough enlarge the holes in its side. A plastic disgorger is useful for doing this adaptation.

- When you cast out a feeder or a leger try to make it enter the water smoothly. If you have clipped up, feather the line – that is just tap your finger against it, to hold it against the spool – and ease the end tackle into the water. This will also put less stress on your line as it won't hit the clip with a sharp thud.

- Sometimes, especially when carp fishing, it might actually work to your advantage to let the feeder splash down! Carp – and sometimes other species – often hear the splash, associate it with food arriving and home in on the noise!

Chapter 5

Great Gizmos

Anglers just love boys' toys! There are some great gizmos around that help make your fishing just a little bit easier. You may already use some of them but there could be others here that make your fishing that bit more enjoyable.

Dosapiombo

No angler likes tying pole rigs and even when you get to the water it's a virtual certainty that you will have to check and adjust the shotting. The dosapiombo helps get around that problem. Neutral density – so that it just floats in water – you clip your float into the top and then place shot or weights on the ledge until the float is pulled down the to required level.

Stotter

Stotz are great little weights for shotting down your float and this specially made pair of pliers lets you clip them on the line easily. It's far better than biting with your teeth!

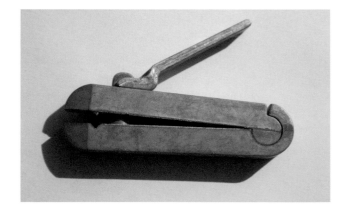

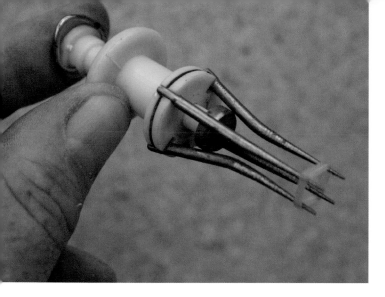

Pellet bander

It can be fiddly and almost impossible to get hard pellets into bands, especially if you have big clumsy fingers. The pellet bander is spring-loaded and can be used to stretch the band just enough for you to slip in a pellet and then allow the band to close around it.

Hook tier

Many anglers prefer to tie spade end hooks by hand but a hook tier is a must for many others. Once mastered this little device will tie perfect knots every time on the smallest to the largest hooks.

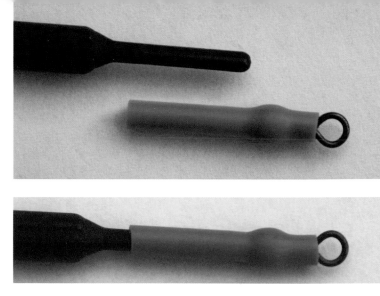

Waggler adaptors fit onto the bottom of the floats and make changing sizes easy

Waggler adaptors

There are many types of waggler float adaptors on the market but the basic principle is the same – they allow you to quickly change your float for a larger or smaller one without breaking down all of your end tackle. A must when float fishing with a bottom end only float.

Paint

Don't worry! It's not for a quick bit of DIY on the bank. Always carry around a small container of float paint, or a paint pen, to help you change the colour of your float tips so that you can see them in different light conditions. The best colours are black, white and fluoro orange.

Net float

How often have you tried to hold your landing net high in the water whilst playing out a fish? A net float, fastened on to the pole near the head of your landing net – usually with Velcro – makes the job so much easier.

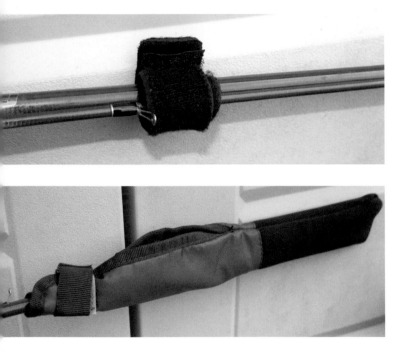

Rod protectors

With the increasing trend of keeping rods made up and just folding them down for transport, rod protectors and bands are a vital part of an angler's kit. You can hold the sections of rod together with these and at the same time also fasten down floats or leads so that rigs don't get trashed.

Method mould

Method feeder fishing can be improved by using a custom-made mould. You fill the mould with the soaked pellets or groundbait you are going to use then push your feeder into the mix. This forms a perfect shape for you to cast. You can bury your hook-bait under that first load of bait, or a second skin, or just fish it loose on a very short hook-length.

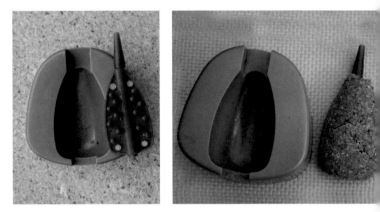

Left: Method feeder and mould.

Right: A neat, aerodynamic ball of groundbait created by the mould with just one squeeze.

Atomiser

One of those plastic containers with a spray that you might use to water plants – only this time it's very handy for just putting a light spray of water on groundbait to get the feed just right. Anglers who fish with bloodworm and joker often use one of these sprays to liven up their baits or keep them just damp.

Pulla bug in place; pull to tighten when you hook a bigger fish and want to land; then hold elastic against your pole – letting it go if the fish decides to run once more.

Puller bungs

A number of manufacturers have different types of puller bung – or even special rollers than can be fitted into the side of your top sections. These are brilliant for helping you to land bigger fish on lighter elastic. Basically, you fish a light or medium elastic that helps you land small fish and when you hook a bigger specimen you break your pole down to the top kit and grab the puller. Then you can pull on the puller to tighten the elastic and get the big fish to the landing net without having to play it out for a very long time. You have to take care not to pull too hard and tighten the elastic too much but with practise it is amazing what you can do with this system.

An atomiser can be used to damp down your groundbait.

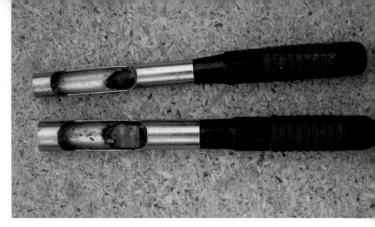

Hook-ups and markers

Hook ups are small rubber bands that push onto your pole and have a little loop into which you can fasten your hook. This is far better than stretching the elastic a long way so that you can put the hook into the bottom section of your top kit. Perfect for when you have plumbed up the depth you want to secure your rig so that it doesn't tangle – and also to know just how deep your float is set in case you lose your rig and have to retackle. Smaller rubber rings (markers), often sold with hook-ups, can be pushed onto the pole and used to mark the depth of your rig. Remember to mark off both top and bottom of your rig against the pole.

Meat punch

Many anglers have used bread punches to stamp out pellets of bait – but meat punches are a very handy tool too! These are usually metal, in the form of cylinders, and come in a variety of diameters. You push the cylinder into a piece of meat and create a hook-bait the size of different pellets. They are easy to put on a hook or a hair and tend to stay on the hook better than bits you tear off a chunk of meat. Sometimes a big chunk of meat is needed and you probably won't find a punch big enough, so will have to revert to cutting the meat with a knife.

Bump bar

A number of anglers struggle to hold a long pole steady – especially when trying to throw or catapult in loose feed. The answer is a bump bar. You can rest your pole on this and sit carefully on the back end of it to hold steady. Many modern boxes come with a slot in the seat and this is where the pole butt should be placed so that you don't actually sit on the carbon fibre and break it! A bump bar also lets you hold a pole steadier in windy conditions or when it is important to hold your bait in one spot without any movement.

Quick stops

Even custom-made stops for use with hair rigs can be fiddly. But quick stops are simple to use and do the same job. You mount these tiny conical shaped stops on a hair rig and push them through your bait with a baiting needle that does not carry a barb. Then you just

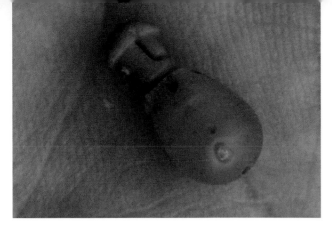

Quick change bead open....

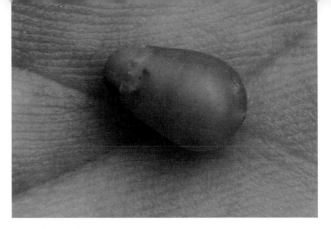

.... and closed

twist the stop so it holds the bait in place. The added bonus is that they don't need replacing every time you land a fish or rebait… which can happen with normal hair stops.

Quick-change beads

You want a longer or shorter hook length, a different breaking strain of line or a different size hook, but can't be bothered breaking down your rig. You don't have to with one of these beads. You slip your hook length out of the bead, which is attached to your main line, and put a new one in the clip. Simple!

Side trays

Not just for anglers who used seatboxes with legs, you can now get side trays that fit to chairs too. Great for keeping bait and small items of tackle to hand and stops all that bending down to reach things stuck on the ground.

Chop scissors

Chopped worm fishing is a super effective way of catching many fish. When you just need to cut up a few big worms it's easy to put them into a pot and snip into bits with a normal pair of scissors. But if you are going to fish the method all day and need lots of worms chopped finely or into various sized pieces you really need a pair of chop scissors. These are like three pairs of scissors all bolted together and do the job in no time at all.

Bait dropper

No angler should be without a bait dropper. It may not be a modern gizmo but this item of tackle is something that can help conquer a multitude of feeding problems. Usually made from metal they are also now available in plastic. They can be tied to your end tackle but, more often than not, they are hooked on to your rig through the small piece of cork on the dropper's body. The door of the dropper can then be opened, bait placed inside, and then it is lowered to the bed of the lake or river. Once its long leg hits the bottom the door opens and the bait spills out. This means deep swims can be fed accurately, even in flowing water. You can use the dropper to also get through hordes of small fish which might intercept loose feed on its way to the bottom. Chopped worm can also be fed through a dropper, something you couldn't do very well if you do not have a pole with a cup attached.

Bait dropper closed...and open

Chapter 6

Watercraft

Good watercraft is vital to making the most of your fishing time. It's something that was hammered home to anglers over the years but many newcomers to the sport in recent decades do not appreciate just how important this skill is to their success.

To most experienced anglers fish-holding swims stick out like a sore thumb. Overhanging trees and bushes, reed beds, lily beds, obstructions in the water… they draw good anglers and fish like a giant magnet. Most of the time fish see this type of place as a sanctuary and quite often they are just waiting there to be caught. But there are other times when features aren't quite so obvious and this is where real watercraft comes into play.

A prime example of this is when you visit what appear to be featureless lakes. In summer there could be trees complete with leaves, rushes lining the banks and fish in most swims. But in winter, floods could lead to paths around the lake being underwater and swims you fished in summer and late autumn now being inaccessible, whilst bank side overhangs and features could have disappeared and many areas now seeming very similar.

Fishing into the wind – if it isn't too cold – has to be a good starting point. The theory being that the warmer surface water will hit the bank you sit on and put warm water, and food, on the table of the fish almost at your feet. The water further into the lake may be a no man's land as it could be deep and would not warm up fast. A margin swim has to be favourite.

Let's look at how I started to fish a lake in winter. I began at 5 metres (16 feet), next to what was left of a tree – just a few branches. Two carp quickly fell to the pole but it didn't feel quite right; the water appeared too deep. Just to the left was another slightly shallower bit of water covering the footpath and some dead rushes where, in summer, I had caught right next to the bank. I plumbed and found it a foot shallower than next to the dead tree, something on this milder day that could attract fish and help with feeding accurately.

A few pellets and dead maggots were fed steadily for the next few hours and that brought 50 fish: 23 carp, the rest skimmers and nice rudd.

Hook baits were chopped and changed between meat, a bunch of maggots and half a big worm, to keep in touch with the fish. A colleague on the other side of the lake sat behind what was normally the path

A lone boat on a stretch of canal – a magnet for attracting all sorts of fish.

and dropped his rig right down what was the edge of the bank. The water was a bit shallower than where I fished, so it would warm up faster, and it was also a place where natural food such as worms would drop into the water. He had around 20 carp too.

In stark contrast, two other anglers who turned up with no boots could only find one spot where they could get near the water. They just tackled up and cast out randomly without even checking the depth. In summer they may have been fishing at around half depth and could have caught. With the extra water they were fishing less than half depth on a cold day.

Neither fed any bait and after an hour without a bite, they disappeared.

A lake can look featureless at first sight – no trees, no rushes, no obvious attractive swims. But a plummet or a leger can show you something totally different. Have a good search around for deeper and shallow holes with the plummet. Look for ledges, plateaus or drop-offs, which are all good fish-holding spots on different days.

A decent sized leger cast out and reeled back in slowly will find gravel or mud, weed beds and obstructions. You can feel a bomb 'rattle' over gravel, pull back a bit as it goes over mud and hit the bottom with a bit of a dull thump when it is mud, soft bottom or shallow.

Think where the natural food will be for the fish. Quite often that is on the shallow shelf at the edges or just at the foot of the slope as the deep water stars. Build up a mental map of the lake's bed and then picture where your quarry might be swimming around feeling they are safe or believing they might find grub. Casting out blind never brings the best results. Spend a bit of time getting to know your swim or venues and it will pay off.

Rules? There are no rules!

Here are five examples of why you should not be a slave to tradition or the rulebook:

Theory: All fish, particularly the likes of chub, just love snags and live under trees and bankside rubbish.

Truth: They often move home! I've now lost count of the times I have actually caught fish away from trees, running a float down the middle of a featureless bit of river or casting to open water in a lake.

Lesson: You can feed fish to get them where you want them. Remember that, just like us, they don't stay at home all day and night.

Theory: Take it little and often with feeding, particularly in the winter.

Truth: I've just heaved in the groundbait – 20 jaffa-sized balls with dead maggots – in cold, clear conditions when feeding like this isn't meant to work. Result… bream and a few roach queuing up for a munch.

Lesson: Just like us, fish get hungry, even when it is cold and we don't expect them to feed. Don't give them small sarnies when they fancy a feast to fatten up for the next cold spell. You've nothing to lose if you weren't getting bites anyway.

Theory: In bright winter conditions you will struggle to catch because fish shelter their sensitive eyes, hiding under cover until the light starts to fade.

Truth: Open water with the sun beating down on it can prove to be far better than shade during winter, and sometimes in summer.

Lesson: The light is sun, sun heats water up, fish like it a bit warmer. A wise old sage once told me that rotting leaves lay on the bottom under a lot of cover in winter and put fish off feeding.

Theory: Moored boats are great places to fish as all species lurk beneath them.

Truth: Boats with black bottoms or hulls are far better than any other colour. I can't explain it! It is always better to fish at the front end rather than the rear – fish know engines are normally at the rear and can spell danger.

Lesson: Don't just fish anywhere if you spot a nice tempting moored craft of any sort. Put a bit of thought into the best spot and always remember to plumb up for holes and shallow spots.

Theory: Light lines and the smallest hook possible will get you far more bites.

Truth: Tricky one this. Sometimes that is the case but not always. What's the point in getting a bite anyway if your hook and line and not up to the job of landing what you tempt into taking your bait?

Lesson: Start as heavy as you dare and scale down until you get bites. Don't start on the lightest and smallest, snap off and possibly ruin sport for the rest of the session. Match baits to hook sizes and never ignore the hair rig.

Don't wear blinkers

Fishing is never quite what you expect it to be at any time of the year. It always pays to take off the blinkers and to experiment – or at least do something you wouldn't normally try and you may catch a few extra fish. Days with clear skies and bright sunshine often mean a run of frosts in winter or very warm temperatures in summer, which are not ideal conditions for catching and you would normally expect fish to feed in shade or near features. But fishing in open water can often given better results, despite those unfavourable conditions. It is possible the fish want that sun on the water to heat it up. Let's look at a couple of real life incidents…

On a small local lake, where fish are normally caught by fishing as close to overhanging brambles as possible, the water was about 1.2 metres (4 feet) deep – a depth that was pretty consistent across the whole venue. Loose feed was trickled into this spot and, as always, I fed another swim, this time with a small amount of fluffy groundbait carrying a few dead maggots. I caught from both areas but the one with the groundbait in open water was best. I fed groundbait in the near swim later in the day but it still didn't fish as well as the swim with no features.

Then, just a few days later, on a local canal where the fish should have been living close to a moored barge, there were only small roach to be caught on pinkie. But a chopped worm line, away from the boat, proved the strongest catching area for nice perch. This line even out-fished the chop line nearest the boat.

On another local lake that is full of features, including bushes, reeds and overhangs, I experimented by going for a swim that offered open water and a feature just to my left. I caught from both areas but the area of open water was once again the best spot. In fact it became solid with fish as I fed steadily!

Same lake, later that week, and a totally open water peg with no features at all. In fact even the depth of water was the same at 3 metres (9 feet) as it was at 8m (26 feet), so there was nothing there to give the fish something to hug, like a ledge or a deeper hole. My peg out-fished everywhere on the lake and I caught a lot more fish than I expected, including carp, tench, perch, rudd and some nice roach.

This proves that all swims need to be tried and should not be written off just because they have no features… and in some cases they should not be shunned because they haven't produced fish before! Fish do not always come from an area right on top of the free bait, groundbait or loose feed. You may catch a few fish over the bait but with cold or bright weather they tend to back off a little just after you have fed or after you have caught a few. Just keep tweaking how you fish, where you fish and what you feed. It could just pay off with a better day than you expected.

Small streams can often hold good fish – and offer lots of features to fish to.

Beat the cold

Winter can see you face much tougher angling conditions. But just because the weather is cold doesn't mean you have to hang up your rods until Spring. There are times in winter when you catch so many fish you wonder what's happened. It's all about timing, getting things right and thinking a lot more about your sport than you did during the warmer months. Chub, grayling and gudgeon will often show in even the very coldest of weathers. Perch, pike, bream and roach are resilient to a frost or two as well. All species have to eat sometime. Don't give up!

Fishing through holes in the ice can produce some fantastic sport. But under no circumstances walk onto the ice and risk your life.

Here are ten tips which could just see you land a few more fish in the cold…

Watch the weather. A river that is coloured but dropping is good. Likewise a settled spell of three days or more of warmer weather will switch on the fish.

Fish light. Fish don't fight as hard in winter, scale down those hooks and line diameters. You will be surprised what you can land on a size 20 hook to just a 700g (1.5 lb) line.

Target species. Don't just cast in and hope. Think about what you are going to catch. Perch will feed in the cold, as will roach, but both like darker days. Bream and skimmers tend to feed in bad weather, especially if there is a bit of colour and ripple.

Fish next to any features, no matter how close to the bank they are.

Eat and drink. You can wait ages in cold weather to get a bite. Make sure you stay alert by eating and having warm drinks.

Feed sparingly. You can't take out what you have already fed, but you can step up the feeding if you start getting more bites. But don't start feeding heavier as soon as you start to get bites. Keep it light or you could find the fish backing off your bait. In fact it's not unusual to get bites, feed and then find the swim dies. Don't dash off home as the fish quite often come back in half an hour or so. Generally speaking, certainly on stillwaters and canals, feed light and then don't put in very much more until you start getting bites.

Worms catch anything. When all else fails the trusty old worm can catch virtually every species. Chop up a few to feed and ensure you fish accurately over the top of the bits. Don't think a small worm or small piece of worm is best… sometimes it pays to go the other way and fish a massive lobworm on the hook.

Casters are a great feed. They lay on the bottom until the fish find them, they can tempt larger fish and other baits can be fished over them. Don't feed too many – they are to fish what eating doughnuts is like for us! Lovely but filling.

Big isn't always best. Small maggots like pinkies and squatts can often catch when bigger maggots fail. Fluoro pinkies fished singly or in doubles can score well over small, hard nuggets of groundbait.

Bright is best – that's baits not your clothing! Sweetcorn and bread can be seen from great distances so in clear winter water they are great baits for fish to home in on. This means you don't have to feed so much.

Don't hammer you swim. If you catch a fish or two from one area, try another spot in your swim to give that spot a rest – or even better change swims if you can.

Feeding correctly

Catching fish in the cold – or even in warmer weather – is all about making the right decisions and being in the right place at the right time. In summer and warmer weather you can make mistakes in presentation, feeding and even swim selection and get away with it. You could still catch a few fish. Get it wrong during winter and you may as well have stayed at home. Get it right and there is nothing like landing a fish you have worked hard for.

Moving until you find feeding fish is a good option. But if you prefer to stay put for longer look for two areas – or even more – of your swim – that you can feed. I'd like three areas and quite often feed four or five areas in a different manner, on flowing water, stillwaters or canals. You can use different baits in each areas, different feed patterns, more or less grub.

My initial ploy would be to have one area that I feed very, very lightly and which I won't necessarily top up until I get a bite or two. Obviously, on flowing water this could mean very little and not so often, usually with the hook-baits, even if I am getting no bites. You need to lure fish to the area, maybe from downstream, or to entice them to feed.

My second area would be a heavier feed area and quite often is a chopped worm and caster line. I'll put in around three chopped lobworms or six to eight dendrobaenas. I won't fish this area for at least an hour after feeding, so that the fish get settled and confident in their feeding. Even then it will be one drop in and if the float doesn't show signs of a bite pretty quickly I will leave the area alone.

Another spot could have a touch of groundbait, fed as small, hard balls, with a few pinkies or dead maggots, and a fourth spot sprinkled with light groundbait with a bit of loose feed put over the top, or maybe a few micro pellets.

If I am fishing the pole I will feed via a pot, even with the loose fed maggots or casters. I like feed tight when the fishing is tough as it tend to pull in a better stamp of fish. If you get more bites sprinkle the feed around a little to give the fish more area to move around in and to compete. This should also lead to you getting better bites.

Use dark groundbaits in clearer water as the fish don't like showing themselves over bright areas, especially when there are predators about. If you think your groundbait isn't dark enough drop some bankside soil in it and give it a good mix to darken it. Make sure you don't get the bait too sticky as you want it breaking up unless it's taking bait to the bottom in flowing water.

Just because it is cold don't presume fish are on the bottom. A bit of warm weather or loose feed will bring them up in the water. Bushes and branches are great on canals – but these areas don't always produce when there are rotting leaves under them.

There's need to get up early – unless you want the pick of spots – because nine times out of ten the last hour of daylight is often the best. My mate and I fished a stretch of river that was clear and low and couldn't buy a bite all day despite dropping to fine lines and tiny hooks with small baits. But as soon as the sun dropped and the light started to fade the river came alive. We stepped up line and hooks and caught no matter what we cast out. It was like a switch had been thrown that said it was feeding time. We'd have caught into dark if we could have seen our floats! Not all days will be like that though so it is important to stay warm, concentrate, don't let the cold get to you and be sure you don't miss those few digs on the quivertip or dips of the float.

General tips

- Fish into the wind. Breezes blow the warm surface water and food articles towards the bank and the fish will follow.

- You trot a float through a river – also give it a try on stillwaters! When there's a good tow on a lake it sometimes pays to let your hook-bait go with the flow to entice a few more bites. Don't let it go too fast though and fish with some line dragging the bottom to slow it down a bit.

- Don't be afraid of raking weed and debris from your swim. The disturbance will colour up the water and dig natural food items out of the silt – which in turn will both attract inquisitive fish, especially carp and tench.

- Ice-breaking on canals and stillwaters can produce some great catches. Smashing the ice and in turn stirring the bottom puts colour in water that would normally be gin clear and this encourages fish to feed.

- Only fish as far out into a lake or river as you can comfortably fish and feed. If you can't cast your float or feeder far enough put on a bigger, heavier one – but remember you may also need to have stronger line on your reel!

- Always wet your hands before holding a fish or your dry, warm skin can removed some of its protective slime. For the same reason never used a cloth or towel to hold your catch.

- Big fish often go on a mad run when they are first hooked. Set the drag on the back or front of your reel so that specimens can pull line from the spool on this charge and not snap you up.

- Don't just try to reel in a decent sized fish. Take your time so that the hook doesn't pull out or the line snap. When you hook a really big fish, pump it steadily towards you by pulling the rod back and then putting the top forward as you reel in line. Never let the line go slack or the fish could slip the hook, but let the fish run when it wants to charge off.

- Change hook-baits regularly, especially when using live baits like maggots and worms. The movement can entice fish to grab the bait – and other baits like meat and corn need to be changed so that you get the maximum from their pulling power of scent and smells.

- Sit or crouch when fishing – don't stand on the skyline as your shadow or silhouette could lay on the water and spook the fish you are trying to catch. If there is any cover like tall grasses and trees use it to your advantage to try and hide your presence.

General repairs

- A centrepin reel is still the best tool for great float control on flowing water and excellent for down the edge fishing on stillwaters. Don't overfill with line, put on just what you need so that it doesn't bed in on itself and you will get a much better performance.

- Watch those pole joints! It's usually the second, third or fourth ferrule that gets the most hammering, especially on put-over poles when it is the male joint that shows wear. You should insert pole protectors but if you don't, or can't, slide an old piece of pole inside the joint, carefully cut it flush and then Superglue in place. This helps repair cracks and makes joints much stronger if you can't afford a new section.

- Clean your pole, inside and out. Wipe down with a soft soapy cloth and clean the insides with a specialist pole cleaning brush – by leaving sections in a bath of water or by pulling/pushing damp kitchen roll carefully through sections.

- Ditch old bait! It's great having a bait fridge and in the long run can save you plenty of cash, but if something has been lurking in there for a long time bin it. Flavours will have leaked away, the bait won't be quite as effective or as tasty and it's a good bet you won't catch as much. Boilies and pellets often become hard or very brittle.

- Clean up reels and replace line that's been on there for any length of time. Any line with knots should be ditched as that's a weakness. Just soak or rub down reels with warm soapy water, allow to dry in a warm room and then give a quick spray or two of WD40. Simple but very effective.

- Go through your bag or box and see what bits and pieces you are missing. Get down to the tackle shop and replace whatever you need – hooks, shot, trace line, swivels – and at the same time throw out anything you haven't used and are not likely to use. It makes boxes lighter and much easier to find things in.

- Check rod rings. In these days of superb guides and great rods at bargain prices it is so easy to forget to check for simple cracks in lined rings or grooves in metal rings. These can soon cut through line and cost you that great fish. Do the same check on bale arm rollers. If you use braid main line it is even more important to make these checks.

- Check both keepnet and landing nets for signs of wear and tear. It's rare now for nets to rot but they could have been snagged on bank-side debris and the mesh torn slightly. Repair simple small holes by using bits of old line if you must – but it's cheap to buy a replacement and might be better in the long run.

- Check your favourite floats. Replace those that have cracks or seal them with paint or a clear varnish. Look at side eyes on pole floats to check they are still firmly in place and replace all rubbers on top and bottom models. Check for loose eyes or swivels on the base of wagglers.

- Never ignore checking your clothing such as overtrousers, jackets and boots. Don't get caught out by cold and damp. We all love clothes that are comfy and fit like a glove, but all clothing eventually needs replacing.

Keep on moving!

Don't just cast out and hope a fish finds your bait. Give whatever's on your hook a bit more attraction with some movement! More times than not most species will immediately intercept baits that are given a bit of a flick, twitch or are dragged a little through your swim. Pegs that appear to be empty of fish suddenly prove you wrong when that maggot, worm or even pellet, caster or corn are lifted a little off the bottom or dragged along the lake, canal or river-bed.

Chub will often take a big bait when all else fails.

Fish – particularly perch – often just hover in the water looking at free offerings on the bottom. Pieces of juicy worm and nice crunchy casters can just be ignored. But when a worm on the hook is lifted an inch off the bottom and then dropped back down again the perch can zoom in to intercept.

Chopped worm fishing often calls for a lot of movement, either lifting the bait slightly and then dropping it back, or even pulling it backwards and forwards through your swim over the baited area. You can actually over-shot your float so that it sinks and then you have to lift it up a touch to bring it back to the surface. Just keep an eye on how fast it sinks or if the float holds up – an unusual movement is a bite.

The late, great Benny Ashurst, father of former World Champion Kevin, often twitched his legered bream baits so much he looked like he was spinning. It wasn't unusual for him to cast out to his feed area and then started slowly inching his bait, almost back to the bank. He caught more than his fair share of bream!

Also lay your rig out on the water, whether you are fishing with a running line or pole. It works best with a pole as you can lay your rig across the surface and then hold it tight as the hook and shot sink through the water. Again you will be amazed at how you sometimes catch fish that you would swore weren't even in your swim.

With a running line float set up you need to cast and then stop the line just before it hits the water so that your hook and shot goes ahead of the float and lays on the water in a similar way to pole fishing.

Chapter 7

Expert Advice

7.1 Taking on the World

Becoming the top performer in any sport is special, but BOB NUDD* has been crowned World Angling champion a staggering *four* times – in 1990, 1991, 1994 and 1999. Bob, who was awarded an MBE for services to angling, represented England for more than 20 years and helped the side win its first World gold medal in 1985 on his second appearance for his country. He went on to win a further seven team golds plus dozens of other medals at international level. But how did he get to the top, and does he have any special secrets?

Did you ever think about becoming World Champion?

Not really! Sometimes in life good fortune puts you in the right place at the right time and you continue from

* Bob Nudd offers coaching sessions, check out his website at www.bobnudd.com. Bob is sponsored by Browning.

there. I won a big match in Ireland – about £3,000 in 1978 I think – and thought 'this match fishing is alright.' Then I won a fair few matches and when Dick Clegg became manager he asked me to fish for England in Switzerland.

How does someone get the chance to be World Champion?

I think the hardest thing is getting the team manager to notice you, so that you can fish for your country. I am sure a lot of anglers would make it if they got there… but having said that it does take an awful lot of effort.

Did you have to make many sacrifices to get to the top?

Not really, not in the same way as other sports. Anglers like a beer and a laugh but you obviously don't socialise as much as some of your friends, because you are out every Saturday and Sunday fishing matches. Your

Bob Nudd is always willing to pass on his knowledge to other anglers.

Bob Nudd with a nice net of mostly roach and hybrids.

family suffers a little too I think, especially if you have young children because you are away from home a lot. It is a very selfish sport but it is also very rewarding.

How much time do you put into preparation for your fishing?

It is difficult to quantify. I don't think you can ever say how much time you put into preparation as you are always doing bits and pieces. It didn't take over my life but angling is very time consuming. Just to fish a match is an all-day event. And for a World Championships it is far more intense, you are not just fishing an individual match. All your teammates are relying on you so you have to make sure that you are 150 per cent prepared so that nothing can go wrong.

What's the difference in fishing a normal five-hour match and the three hours of competition for a World Championship?

You have to make sure you are on the ball from the word go for the World matches. Sometimes in a normal match you can spend time getting the fish going for an hour and you still have another four hours in which to win. But in a world champs if you are not catching early or are not in a good rhythm you can be in trouble. It is quite intense.

What was it like winning your first World title?

It was fantastic because I was the new kid in the team even though I had been there for about six years. I was still a bit like the junior member of the side. It was a very difficult match, fished on a very powerful and deep river in the former Yugoslavia. In practice both Kevin Ashurst [teammate] and I would come out top or second and I felt very confident and at ease. I won my section both days of the championship to take the title and Kevin was second.

No matter what the weather you will find Nuddy on the bank.

A pole-caught roach is swung to hand by Bob Nudd during a match in Ireland.

Which one of the four wins do you remember most?

All were fantastic. You feel honoured to represent your country first of all and to win is the icing on the cake. Holme Pierrepont in Nottingham [1994] was difficult fishing but we had a very partisan crowd – there were thousands of people and I had never seen so many at a fishing match. The last one in 1999 [Spain] was also special as that was a real fishing match with lots of fish and I still hold the record of having caught the heaviest weight in any World Championship, which was more than 50kg (110lb) over the two days. Hungary [1991] I again won my section both days with lots of small fish… they are all rewarding wins.

What do you think when you look back now at having won that title four times?

I still believe I was in the right place at the right time and knew what to do. I never think I am the best in the world and all that rubbish. Good fortune put me there and it was the right style for me on the day.

How did the wins change your fishing, with so many people now wanting to watch you fish and check out your methods?

As they are anglers they just talk and laugh and if you get beat they love it. It's never bothered me. Then I have always used the media well because my philosophy is that without people writing and talking to you no one knows who you are. It is no good being the best angler in the world if no one knows! I never worry about getting beaten, I am never big-headed about it because the actual fishing is the most important part about the sport.

Who do you look up to in angling?

To mix with top anglers, which I did at World Championships, was so important. In the beginning it was Kevin Ashurst and Ian Heaps [World Champions individually and team-wise with England]. Later on it was England colleagues Steve Gardener and Alan Scotthorne. Everyone learns something from each other and I am still learning. That is why fishing is so exciting to me.

What's the most important thing for anglers to remember?

Without getting the fish in your swim and getting them feeding you can't catch them. Feeding accurately is important too. I am always looking at little things trying to improve, making small adjustments to my tackle and rigs.

When you take people fishing, what's the question they ask you most?

It's not the most asked question, but most anglers are surprised when they see me feeding and say, 'I never did that, I've never seen this' – then they catch 200lb [90kg]. You tell them that when they are on fish you have to work out how much to feed. They don't ask the question because they don't know to ask it. The most important thing to instill into anglers is to feed. It varies on every venue but I tell them that if they learn how to do that on the places they fish they will catch more, or will win matches.

7.2 Fishing the unknown

You are about to fish a decent-sized natural lake but haven't been able to find out much about it other than it contains carp, bream, roach and a few tench. You don't know the depth but there are a few trees, overhanging bushes, lily pads and the wind is blowing towards one end. It's a bright day but not too sunny. How do you fish this venue? That's the poser MARK POLLARD* was given.

MARK POLLARD has been one of England's top anglers for more than two decades. He's been in the top ten Matchman of the Year ratings for most of that time and won the trophy once. Highly rated on canals, Mark has also won many events on lakes and rivers on many methods.

What bait and gear would you take along and why?

I would have worms, casters, red maggots and some fluoro pinkies. I will also have micro and expander pellets. Pellets work on all lakes and natural venues. Unlike in the past I can now catch big weights on canals, rivers and lakes using pellets rather than normal baits as people who fish commercial venues use the

* Mark Pollard can be booked for coaching sessions through www.markpollardfishingdays.com. He is sponsored by Shimano and Dynamite Baits.

stuffed full of fish that were churning up the bottom looking for food!

Which area of the lake are you looking to fish and why?

I would look for overhanging trees and any cover on the inside – providing it is not sedges and it is 3 feet [1 metre] deep and clear. There would be no fish in that clear water. Always fish into the wind, the end of the lake the wind is blowing into is always the better end. The sun isn't really a factor – but if the sun is in your face it can be a pain when you are fishing the pole as you may not be able to see your float. But if you are on the quiver tip the sun doesn't matter so much as you can angle the rod so you can still see bites.

How would you fish?

I would set up my feeder rod but with just a bomb on the line and cast out to about 30–40 yards [27–36 metres] to check what the depth is by counting the leger down to the bottom. A count of one is roughly a foot deep, two is two feet etc. I would retrieve the leger slowly to see if there was any rubbish, snags or weed on the bottom. If the area is clear I would clip up the line and empty eight or nine medium feeder fulls of bait to the same place in that far swim. This would contain groundbait with a few casters and a bit of chopped worm. After feeding that far line I would start fishing the pole line, which I would already have fed by balling in groundbait. This natural venue mix would include one bag of Dynamite Baits Frenzied Hemp Matchblack, a third of a bag Natural Roach Silver X

same baits everywhere. I would have a couple of feeder rods, a waggler rod and a pole.

Are you going to target any specific species?

If the water looked clear it would tell me that it is not heavily stocked with fish and I would have a feeder and long pole approach. If the water was very coloured I know it can't be a great depth otherwise it would be

feeder line. I would stay on that pole line for at least 40 minutes before going out on the tip as I want the fish on that far line to settle and feed confidently over that bait I put out at the start.

Do you aim for quality or quantity?

I would look to be catching on the feeder and see what I can catch. If I was there practising for a match the next day I would look to see what the best method was to catch fish. It may be I catch a few perch on the feeder but not so many on the pole. The species I catch will give me my tactics.

If you get no bites having tried your first methods what do you decide to do to get out of jail?

I would probably set up a waggler rod, feed just a few casters and fish a little bit further out than my pole line. I would have light shotting down the line so that the maggot on my hook drops slowly through the water giving me a chance to catch any fish at any depth. I want to catch anything that swims and this would give me the best chance. I would also feed chopped worm in an area of my swim as many venues hold perch – and as we all know perch just love worms! I would also be looking at scaling down my end tackle to a size 20 hook and 0.08mm line, which is about 1lb [450g] breaking strain.

and a third of a bag of browncrumb. This would also contain a few casters and chopped up worms. I would loose feed a few caster over the top.

How would you see the session progressing?

If I am catching on the pole I will stay on that method. But if the bites started to dwindle a bit I would cup in a few balls of groundbait and then have a cast to the

It's nearly time to go home but you think there is a chance of a late run of fish. How do you try to make it happen?

If I were catching on the feeder I would cut back on the particles in the groundbait – in this case the chopped worm and casters. That way the fish would have to grab the bait on my hook. This could also knock sport on the head as you are not giving them the particles they are trying to search out – but it could also give you that late run of fish.

Do you write down what you have learnt so you remember any lessons?

No, I always log the information in my head. But I might get home and tie up some hooks to line and prepare some pole rigs so that next time I visit that venue I have the right gear in my tackle box. You can waste a lot of time on the bank sorting out things like that – and in a match situation that could cost you that one vital fish that would win you the event! Just think how many fish it could also cost you in a pleasure fishing session if you spend 15 minutes sorting out gear on the bank!

You take quite a few anglers out for coaching sessions to help them improve their fishing. What's the question you are asked most?

How do you feed? It is always about feeding… when to feed, how much and where to put it. So many anglers just don't know. It is a simple thing but put it together with everything else you learn and you will catch. It is not something that is easy to explain to someone. Feeding is something that comes naturally through time, trial and error. The more times you go fishing the more you will get to understand this subject.

7.3 Tactical thinking

DAVE COSTER, Product Innovation Manager for Pure Fishing, has been answering readers' questions for *Angler's Mail* magazine for over 20 years. One of the most common enquiries he receives is how to sort out the best tactics for each new session. These are his thoughts to that puzzler.

A lot of experienced anglers would say that finding the best catching method is down to watercraft and experience, but I would argue that even experienced anglers don't always get it right!

That's why you need to keep an open mind and be prepared to change tactics quickly if your initial plan isn't working. As a match angler, my constant aim is to get things sorted as quickly as possible, because every minute that goes by without catching anything is going to make it more and more difficult to win!

But the same guidelines that I use in match fishing can also be applied to get the best out of your swim when pleasure fishing.

There are lots of little pointers that can help. If the water is coloured there's a better chance of catching fish close in on the pole. If the water is clear the pole is likely to spook fish very quickly so running line tactics could be a better bet.

If early signs show there's a lot of fish in a peg, the best way to catch a big weight will be to get them feeding as close in as possible. If the fish are competing for feed (signalled by bites on the drop, as your bait falls through the water) the obvious solution is to fish shallow.

A huge bag of prime roach for Dave Coster.

Dave Coster slips the landing net under a nice roach.

If bites are hard to come by with a bait that is on the bottom, suspending hook offerings an inch or so just off the bottom is more likely to induce a take from lethargic fish.

A good way to highlight how different sessions and venues dictate different approaches is to recount some match and pleasure outings.

Recently I was one of the front runners in an individual league. I needed a good result on the penultimate round, but drew a shallow area where not many match-winning skimmers tend to show up.

The first hour was a nightmare. Plenty of bites on everything I tried but I missed many of them on the feeder, long pole and waggler, mainly because the swim was infested with small gudgeon, roach and perch.

The way it was going it was hard to see anything better than a target weight of 4–5 lb [1.8–2.2kg], which with deeper skimmer pegs included in the match would be a long way off the mark.

So I quickly brought a four metre whip into play and decided to go for numbers instead of quality. It was hard work catching more than 300 fish during the next four hours but it paid off big time. I beat the league leader on the next peg, weighing in 11lb 14oz [50.75kg] for second in the match.

A few weeks later fishing on an Open match on the same venue I drew the deeps where normally it's skimmers or bust on the feeder. However, I noticed a nice tinge of colour in the water and also saw lots of roach topping in the area.

Bearing in mind that skimmer sport had been a bit patchy on the lake over recent weeks, I decided to take a gamble and go straight on the whip again.

It worked a treat and by the time others cottoned on to what I was doing, I was miles ahead, catching a nice stamp of roach and at a steady rate.

A small ball of groundbait every cast, laced with a few casters, using red maggot on the hook did the trick. I ended up with 200 roach for 18lb 8oz [8.39kg] and a clear win.

But there is a downside to this story. I drew the peg next door two weeks later and couldn't get a bite on the same rig! By the time I got on the feeder other anglers around me were catching skimmers and I couldn't get a bite! I'd fallen into the blinkered trap and got a very rude awakening!

I can give you another interesting insight into how to search out the fish, although in this instance the particular venue took a fair time to crack.

I'd heard through the grapevine that there are some big roach in a game fishing reservoir near where I now live in Northumberland. I have a good relationship with Northumberland Water Authority, so I asked them if I could fish the place after it closed to the game anglers late last year.

They let me on there for a month and to begin with it was a right puzzle. I caught a few good roach on the feeder at varying distances, trying different areas, but a similar pattern emerged where bites quickly dried up.

I also tried the pole at various lengths but that produced much the same results – a quick flurry of activity then nothing. I was beginning to think maybe there weren't that many roach in the place.

I kept at it though and on one particular session I discovered a slight drop off 20 metres out, running several hundred yards along the north bank of the reservoir.

If I cast a feeder out I could feel it bumping into this feature on the way in. I also noticed that out in the open water there were quite a few cormorants hunting fish, which made me think that maybe the roach would be close to the ledge – the only real feature in the place.

But trying to drop a feeder near the ledge didn't work. There were lots of snags down there and if I went just past them, any hooked fish dived straight into the rubbish.

This made up my mind to try a waggler, set at a depth just above the debris around the ledge area. I balled in groundbait laced with casters to start and then loose fed over the top with red maggots.

It was suddenly a different world and I caught quality roach from 8oz [226g] up to the 1lb 8oz [680g] and they kept on coming for most of my remaining sessions. Magic!

Finally, regarding sorting out winning tactics, now I live up north it's very different to my old haunts down in the south of England. One of my favourite southern techniques for silver fish was to fish the pole to the left and right of my peg, aiming to get quality roach feeding just down the ledge, which was normally around 7 or 8 metres out. The thinking behind this was if one feed area gets disturbed, it gives the opportunity to switch to another and keep catching at a good rate.

I used this method on several venues and one occasion won a match at Gloucester Park in Basildon with a mighty 56lb [25kg] haul of quality roach!

However, I just can't make this work on venues where I fish now. I can catch big weights of similar size roach but find I have to fish further out for them and over just one feed line, which is usually around 12 to 13 metres.

The trick here is to have several pole rigs set up at varying depths. The session is started at full depth but the plan is with regular feeding to draw the fish up in the water. This is where the bigger fish tend to show but you need to fish very light for them, using 0.08mm hook lengths and tiny size 20 fine wire hooks with baits like maggots, casters or tares.

Perch and roach from a wild northern reservoir for Dave Coster.

I haven't yet broken the 50lb [22kg] barrier but have come close to 40lb [18kg] quite a few times. I'm still mystified why the better quality fish won't come closer into the nearside ledge, but it underlines to me how important it is keeping an open mind at all times.

The way I look at it is each fishing session is like a game of chess. You can have a set opening move but very often the next step needs to be instinctive, certainly if you are going to get the best out of every swim you fish.

7.4 On the pull

JASON LE BOSQUET* is a former UK Angling Champion. But he will also be forever remembered for landing a monster 64lb (29kg) sturgeon on a pole. Here are his tips for landing big fish and big weights on the pole.

Looking back over the past decade of match fishing, it is unbelievable how things have changed and moved forward, from catching 20–30lb [9–13kg] of silver fish to catching 100lb [45kg] of carp and F1s.

However, over the last few years even these weights been surpassed and now it is not uncommon to need 200lb-plus [90kg] to frame in a match and a 'mere' 100lb [45kg] will only win a section prize at best.

In my opinion, this is down to a few things, including tackle, the way we play fish and also the change of opinions in the way we balance out tackle.

I know it opened quite a few eyes when I caught a British record fish on a normal match pole. This sturgeon was 64lb and, even for myself, a matchman with more than 25 years' of experience, this was a real eye opener to what can be landed on balanced match tackle.

The tackle breakdown when I caught this huge fish was a 16m Garbolino Power Legion Pole, 0.21mm to 0.19mm Garbo line, a size 12 GammaPower hook and a 14-16 rated hollow elastic.

The fish took 1 hour and 15 minutes to land but during that time – at least after the first quarter of an hour – I was confident of landing the beast.

* Jason Le Bosquet is sponsored by Garbolino.

Pulla kits help Jason Le Bosquet land big nets of fish in a shorter space of time.

Over the past couple of years I have lost count of the amount of times I have caught 120–170lb [54–77kg] of fish using nothing heavier than a 10–12 hollow elastic and 0.15mm main line to 0.13mm hooklengths with a size 16 hook. This is mainly down to the evolution of the Pulla bung or side Pulla kits which allow you to strip elastic from inside your pole and massively reduce the amount of time that it takes to land a big fish on lighter elastic.

A nice carp from the margins for Jason.

My tackle nearly always incorporates top kits with Pullas and hollow elastics. The simple reason for this is that when you use this set up the fish – no matter how big or small – can be hooked and caught without the fear of breaking your pole. There is also little worry about the hook pulling out of the fish because your elastic is simply too strong or set too tight in the pole.

For instance, if you are catching 8–10oz [220–285g] fish on a hollow 4-6 elastic and you hook a 5lb [2.2kg] carp, then the chances are that you will get this bonus fish out as you have enough stretch in your elastic and strength in your line to cope.

Additionally, because you are fishing with Pulla kits it will not take you too much time to get the fish into your net.

All these valuable minutes that we can save by landing fish quicker, means that we get more time during a match with our rig actually in the water. This gives us more opportunity to get more bites and catch more fish, and therefore putting a bigger weight on the scales come the end of the match.

As a general rule of thumb I will fish a carp match in summer with 0.15mm mainline to 0.13mm hooklengths in open water matched with a 10-12 hollow elastic and a size 16 hook.

Jason Le Bosquet with his 64lb sturgeon – the biggest fish caught on a pole in the UK.

For my fishing area at five metres, and margin swim where I could look to be catching 100lb-plus in the last hour, I will fish 0.19mm mainline to 0.17mm hooklength and a size 12 or 14 hook to a 14-16 hollow elastic.

In my eyes, this is balanced tackle and I would not be worried about catching fish from 2lb to 20lb [0.9kg to 9kg] on this gear.

It is also important to play a fish correctly if you want to land it safely, and in a relatively fast time. Personally, after I hook a fish I like to make sure that in the first few seconds I am happy that the fish is hooked properly, not foul hooked somewhere other than in the mouth!

Once I believe the hook hold is good, I let the fish run into the lake whilst carefully shipping back my pole. At all times I will be aware that if the fish bottoms out my elastic I need to ship my pole back out again and follow the fish until it is back under my control.

When I feel that I am in control of the fish I will again ship back my pole to my top kit, break down the pole and start stripping elastic from my side puller.

When I have stripped back sufficient elastic from the top kit and the fish comes to the surface I quickly tilt my arm to a 45-degree angle behind my head and scoop the fish into the landing net.

7.5 Make the most of your margins

DARREN COX* is one of the best allround anglers in England and has represented his country ten times. He has a host of big finals under his belt and has no less than ten team and individual medals from National Championships.

There is no nicer way of catching big carp on commercials than seeing them appear in your margin swim after spending a few hours feeding that area like your life depended on it.

The anticipation is fantastic as you drop in with your margin rig and hope that you hook the fish and it's a great big one! The only feeling better than hooking that first one is when you get another one the very next put in!

We spend a long time feeding our margins often only to catch one or two at the very end of a session or competition but it really does make it all worthwhile and can be the difference between winning and being an also-ran.

There are lots of ways to approach your margin swims and as commercial fishing has developed so too have the tactics as fish get bigger and wiser. In the warmer months, when the water temperature is a lot higher and the fish are eating much more, it is normal to expect to feed a lot of bait to encourage them to stay in the margins and eat. In fact all we think we are doing is replicating what normally happens when an

* Darren Cox is sponsored by Garbolino and fishes for the crack Starlets outfit.

angler packs up – he usually throws all his waste bait in the edges rather than take it home.

The fish have become wise to this and often respond to the noise of a lot of bait going in. They have become accustomed to finding these treasure troves of bait later in the day and get into the routine of 'patrolling' the margins at that time.

The problem is when we throw pints of particles into a margin and it only attracts an odd fish, then they become extremely difficult to catch as they gorge themselves on the ridiculous amounts of feed. Then the chances of foul-hooking the fish become much greater than actually hooking them in the mouth, which is not good as most of the time you will lose them. If there are lots of fish then it's not a major problem but we have now found a way of mimicking a lot of bait going in without actually overfeeding the swim, however many fish may turn up.

This is by feeding mainly groundbait and controlling the amount of particles in it depending on the response from the fish. The groundbait is very fine and has little food content but it looks like a lot of bait in the swim which attracts the fish in the first place.

As long as there are a few particles mixed into the groundbait the carp will happily sift through this feed for long periods of time. The groundbait even helps form clouds in the water which in turn helps us as anglers as the fish will feel more confident the more coloured the water is where they are feeding. This disturbance will also attract more fish into the swim.

To kick the swim off at the start I put one or two large pole pots full of groundbait into my margins. In these pots there will be a few particles of maggots,

casters or corn depending on what you feel the fish will prefer to eat on the day.

I feed when I expect to start catching down the margin. If I don't believe the fish will want to move into the margins until two hours from the end of the match I won't bother feeding much there until then.

Remember we are trying to create that 'packing up' effect so it's better to feed a lot all at once when the carp are ready to eat it. Feed before this and you are likely to be feeding the silvers and bits, which live in the margins all day, then when the carp turn up there will be no bait for them and they will move off.

Often the tell-tale vortex of a carp wafting its tail in the surface tension is all you need to set your heart racing as you realize that there are feeding fish exactly where you want them.

Generally, because they are feeding fish, you can get away with a decent size hook and line. If I am targeting commons and mirrors then I will want to fish a size 12 or 14 strong hook tied to 0.18mm or even 0.20mm Garbolino rig line. Floats have to be small (0.10g or 0.20g) but strong and robust with thick buoyant tips so that you can determine the slower liners from the fast 'bang under' true bites.

Only lift at these true bites and you will avoid the foul hooked fish. The floats I prefer are the Garbolino DCX3 or DCX4 patterns which stand up to the job well.

Where you expect big fish then don't mess about, make sure you have strong enough elastic to keep them under control quickly otherwise they will kite out and take some retrieving! Garbolino Bazookarp COEX hollow elastic in 2.5mm or 2.7mm diameters is perfect when fitted to a puller kit system.

Hook baits have to be large and visible so the carp will pick them out in the cloud created from the groundbait and mud the fish stir up.

Bunches of dead maggots, even as many as 12 on the hook, are deadly, or one or two large dendrobaenas.

These hook baits will be found quickly when the fish are feeding well and that means more fish in the net rather than foul hooking them. Meat and corn also work well but the above two baits are the killers over ground bait.

Remember you may have to keep piling the groundbait in after every fish as the big fish can often waft this feed out of the swim very quickly and you will need to replicate the 'packing up' scenario once again. Where groundbait is not allowed you can create the same effect with micro pellets or liquidised corn, just remember that you don't want to feed the fish too much, enough to keep them in the swim until they end up on the hook!

In the warmer weather always look for 300mm–500mm of depth as close to the bank or a feature like a bush or reeds (or ideally both). In colder weather the best depth may be as deep as 1 metre [3 feet] and away from the bank a little as the bigger fish may be reluctant to expose themselves in clearer water and cold conditions.

When the water is colder a more subtle approach is often needed. This is where I leave my groundbait at home and opt for smaller particles such as corn, casters and maybe even a few pellets.

Forget the big pots as the carp react totally differently in the cold and become a lot less active and a lot more cautious. Little and often feeding is much better as I now want to catch all those small fish as well as they may be vital by the end of a match.

Smaller hooks and bait will mean that I can take advantage of the smaller fish but also have a chance to land any carp which come along later in the day as they will be a lot more sluggish and much easier to land even on light tackle. Lighter 1.8mm hollow elastics will be perfect teamed up with diameter 0.14mm or even 0.12mm Garbo Line hook lengths and size 16 or 18 Kamasan B911 hooks.

Remember to always match the hook size to the bait size, the hook gauge and line diameter to the size of the fish you expect to catch.

The time of year obviously has a big effect on how well you catch in the margins and in the height of summer the fish will be itching to move into the shallows as soon as they feel it is safe, on overcast warm and windy days you may find them there from the start of session whatever time of day it is.

Sometimes even in winter the fish may be in shallow water trying to find the correct thermoclines to suit their mood.

I will always feed my margin swims whatever the time of year as you never really know what to expect, and one fish can make a big difference.

Whether you are having a nice day enjoying yourself pleasure fishing, on your local club match with a group of friends or fishing for £25,000 in a televised big open match, the margin line is often what I call 'the final piece of the jigsaw' in your fishing session; get it right, be patient and you will be pleasantly rewarded at the end and go home with a big smile on your face.

7.6 Ten tips for catching more big carp

COLIN DAVIDSON is an experienced carp angler, instructor, fisheries lecturer and qualified angling coach, having caught carp to over 40 lb [18kg] both at home in England and abroad. During more than 25 years of angling he's fished venues as varied as canals, rivers, gravel pits and commercial fisheries and has a carp angling column every week in Angler's Mail magazine.

One of the best sights around, a superb common carp.

Big, hard-fighting and with an ability to learn from experience apparently beyond that of other species, carp have captured the imagination of anglers everywhere. Able to survive and thrive in waterways

Never ignore the shallow margins when fishing for carp.

as diverse as colossal gravel pits, brackish tidal river systems, canals and even the tiniest farm ponds, carp are no longer the uncatchable, mystery species of previous generations. Found the length and breadth of the United Kingdom and in most parts of Europe, carp have become the mainstay of the coarse fishing scene. They look good, fight hard and present an exciting challenge.

There has never been a better time to catch big carp, and whether tackling energetic smaller carp that can be found in almost any commercially managed stillwater, or targeting the biggest, most elusive and challenging fish that can take years of dedication to catch, the basic

Put in the work and you too can catch superb carp like this one to Colin Davidson.

requirements remain the same. Enigmatic they may be, but carp are no harder to catch than any other coarse fish – and with the huge explosion of specialist tackle, tactics and bait aimed specifically at carp it's easier than ever to go and connect with one of the biggest and most powerful fish in fresh water.

1. Feet and inches

More so than almost any other coarse fish species, carp are found most often in the margins. Modern carp angling is obsessed with rods and reels that will cast huge distances, yet even on the biggest waters carp can routinely be found and caught just inches from the bank. Even where bankside noise and disturbance is a common feature carp still gravitate towards the edges, simply melting away to quieter margins, or those where access is more difficult for the angler.

Colin Davidson takes his time to land a nice carp.

2. Get on top

Carp love to be in the upper layers, and it's hard to miss the big dark shapes of carp as they cruise just below the surface on hot and bright days. Almost all carp will keenly feed on floating baits, so always carry surface tackle to exploit any opportunities. Just a small bag of floating trout pellets, a few controllers, some line grease and small hooks are all you need to catch very big carp that other anglers are ignoring. Don't happily sit behind silent bite alarms catching nothing on baits presented on the bottom when all the carp can clearly be seen sunning themselves.

A steady introduction of floating baits will often see carp compete keenly for the offerings as soon as more are fired out, and your first cast can result in a hooked carp. There's nothing to beat the excitement of watching a big pair of carp's lips engulf your hook bait!

The first place to look for carp is always under your feet, which means the angler able to approach the water stealthily without elephant-like footfalls can find, watch and often catch carp in places that most anglers wouldn't even take a second glance at.

No matter how busy a fishery, always get into the habit of feeding a handful or two of bait around margin features and leaving the area for an hour or two for carp to find the feed and build their confidence. Carefully lowering a rig over the top can be a quick way to catch carp that other anglers are casting well beyond.

3. Bright and beautiful

Carp have a fascination with bright coloured baits. Probably through curiosity carp often come and investigate almost anything that is brightly coloured, and a bright bait either on its own or in combination with a darker one is a great way of attracting a carp's attention and bringing extra action. Either use small, bright pop-ups in conjunction with standard boilies, or try one of the many varieties of brightly coloured grains of plastic sweetcorn that are available. Yellow, white and pink are the most consistently effective

Don't miss out on early morning carp sessions.

colours – but the carp can prefer one colour one day, and a different colour the next!

4. Good times

Time is as critical as place when it comes to catching carp. Many anglers miss the potentially most productive times of the 24-hour cycle, reducing their chances of catching considerably.

Turning up at 8am during high summer has seen you miss almost four hours of daylight, and in those first hours of the day carp have often been very active, fed hard and will then spend much of the rest of the day digesting their morning feed.

Arrive too late and you are fishing for odd chances not lots of active, busy carp. Pack up late afternoon and you might miss another feeding spell as the day cools towards dusk and the carp switch on again.

Changing the timing of your fishing trips is a quick way to see if your fortunes take a turn for the better. The first and last few hours of the day often see carp at their most active in the warmer months, through

Lower your baits gently into the margins.

the winter action tends to be later in the day or into darkness.

5. Watch and learn

The skill common to all the very best anglers – whether they are match, carp or fly fishing experts is good observation. You have to learn to look for the clues carp give you that show where they are and what they are doing.

Carp are the easiest of all coarse fish to spot because of their size. From jumping and rolling through to coloured water in the margins, or sheets of bubbles amongst weedbeds and knocking lily stems or reeds the signs are there to be seen. Learn not to set up in the 'favourite' swims or one where you caught a fish a few weeks ago. Instead get into the habit of looking around and only choosing a spot when you are sure you have seen signs of carp. Sitting in the wrong swim because you didn't look around is the most common cause of a blank carp trip, and always will be.

6. Catching not camping

Setting up a bivvy and settling down behind baited rods for the night has a huge excitement and anticipation that isn't found in match or pleasure fishing. But for many anglers night fishing proves to be a distraction rather than a benefit. Pitching camp for several days requires a lot of tackle and equipment to keep you comfortable, well fed and watered – from beds to sleeping bags, stoves, cookware and coolbags.

Several shorter day trips will almost always result in more chances and better results than making camp in one swim for several days at a time. Concentrating on day sessions, or even shorter trips such as afternoons, or early mornings teaches you to go looking for carp and to fish for them where you see them rather than setting traps and waiting.

7. All together now

Where you find one carp there will almost always be lots of them. A very social species, carp can be found in large numbers even in very small areas. It's a double-edged sword, because if most of the carp tend to be in the same place that leaves lots of areas of a fishery where there are very few fish. It's the reason why one or two anglers often appear to be catching plenty but just a few swims away others are struggling for a bite.

Where you see signs of carp there are likely to be lots of them together. You might see just one or two carp roll or crash, but that could mean there are 50 other big carp in the same area that you can't see. If you put your efforts into looking for signs of carp and fishing there, the hardest part of the battle is won.

8. Rig reality

Simplicity is the most important ingredient for successful carp rigs. Remember, a simple rig will catch an even difficult-to-fool carp if you put an attractive bait in a place where the fish is happy to feed. The most complicated rig catches nothing if it is in the wrong place or a carp doesn't want the bait you are offering. Today's ready-made rigs from major manufacturers are a great starting point, and also give you something to copy when you are confident to tie them yourself. A sharp, strong hook on a short 6–8 inch (15–20cm) length of soft braid is a simple and very reliable go-anywhere carp-catching rig.

9. Chopping and changing

Vary what you use for hook baits to try and find something that the carp get caught on more readily. The same carp that doesn't enthusiastically eat your boilie will often wolf down a big bunch of maggots – and that can be the difference between blanking and catching. There are so many options and you should always be trying to find a winning formula – whether it is a hair-rigged pellet, boilie wrapped in paste, bright white pop-up, plastic corn or a piece of spicy sausage. Changing hook baits is a simple and deadly way to get bites, and you'll find out very quickly when you've

Even in winter it's possible to find good carp fishing.

cast out if you have discovered the winning formula – often you will catch within minutes not hours.

10. Cycle of success

The only way to become a better carp angler is by catching carp! Don't try and run before you can walk by aiming for huge carp from difficult venues. If you are a newcomer, concentrate on waters where there are plenty of fish. Sitting on a venue where captures are very occasional will teach you nothing and most likely put you off fishing totally.

Commercially run fisheries offer the chance of regular action, and these are the venues where you can develop skills in every department from accurate casting to regular feeding; to competent night fishing; to handling, weighing and unhooking carp safely. These venues offer a great incentive to improve your abilities – because when you get things right you'll quickly be catching more fish than everyone else around you.

7.7 Getting the best from your swim

HARRY BILLING is one of England's most consistent team and individual performers. He has won a number of big-money individual events in the UK but also has gold medals from the Division One National, Super League and Winter League. He is a consultant for Garbolino.

Harry Billing with a nice net of match-size carp.

What's the biggest mistake you see anglers make whilst they are fishing commercial venues?

The most common mistake is almost always regarding correct feeding. This is one of the hardest things to get right and can change on a daily basis. As a general rule I normally err on the side of caution especially on tightly pegged matches, or when it has been cold. Don't always assume that the fish are ravenous and ready to eat everything that you throw at them.

I would normally start a session by catapulting or throwing two or three pellets depending how far you are fishing out, every two minutes and take it from there. If the fish respond then you can up the feed accordingly, but in my experience the fish normally like to be drip-fed and dumping bait is a no-no. Don't forget most commercial lakes are stuffed with fish and when you sit down at your peg they are already in front of you. They just need coaxing into feeding. Watch out for changes in temperature and wind prior to the session and adjust your feeding accordingly, I've seen many a peg ruined by too much initial feed. Remember you are trying to coax the fish into feeding, it's better to start off with small amounts and try and gauge the response.

What's your secret for getting those few extra fish in big matches – the ones that make the difference between winning and losing?

I've been fortunate to qualify for a lot of big matches, and my finest moments have been in the Parkdean

Masters, which I have won on two occasions and finished third twice. On both winning performances I targeted everything that swims – and to me that means fishing worms. The final is fished on Jenny's Lake at the fabulous Whiteacres complex in Cornwall and is stuffed with fish from 1oz [28g] to 15lb [6.8kg]. I fished at 13 metres [42 feet] and fed the peg through a small pot on the end of my pole. By catching silver fish and carp I was able to keep putting fish in my net and by snaring a few bonus carp was able to triumph. Happy days!

Match anglers are noted for fishing more than one area of their pegs. How do you go about doing that?

This is a fact! During a match it is very rare to keep catching fish from one area of your swim as the fish will shy away from that same spot. I normally have at least four or five areas of my swim primed in case I need to make a switch because the fish have become finicky. As a very general rule I would have lines for a feeder, long pole and short pole, plus two areas down the edge. I would be prepared to try each swim as I thought necessary. A really good tip is if you catch a few fish and then you foul hook one then it is time to make the switch. In my experience to persevere in that area will result in missed bites and more foul hooked fish. Give the area a rest but keep on drip feeding the spot to try again later.

What would you say to somebody who really wants to improve on their angling or match fishing?

My biggest advantage over a lot of anglers is that I use a spray bar and a backshot. The spray bar allows me to keep my pole and rig steady and gives me more control over the float, especially when fishing long in a strong wind. This is made a lot easier with a quality pole, I use a Garbolino Super Legion, and it really is a phenomenal piece of kit. I'm not the biggest or strongest person and I'm certainly not getting any younger, but I find the spray bar an absolute must. Combining the spray bar and the backshot is a killer combination. The difference in presentation is unbelievable and I'm convinced it has enabled me to win a lot more matches. The backshot can be anything from a No.8 to a swan shot, depending on the conditions. It is normally placed about a foot above the float and is held under the surface of the water. It basically acts as a dampener to the movement of the pole in the wind. I always use a wire stemmed float in the wind, something like a Garbolino DC18. As a very rough guide you should use 0.1gm per foot of water, so if the depth is five foot I would use a float that carries 0.5gm.

When you go to a venue – even one you have visited before – how do you know which method to use and what to fish for?

It is essential to ask lots of questions about what was caught on the last match – or if you are pleasure fishing what's being getting caught and where. The best person to ask is the fishery owner or bailiff. Having the right info is a must but don't be afraid to try your own different methods.

I see a lot of anglers come down to Cornwall to fish matches near where I live and they do really well

Proof that the pole doesn't just land small fish, a nice common for Harry Billing.

on methods which we locals wouldn't normally use. For example a lad comes down from Swindon every year and catches loads of fish on dead maggots fished at three metres.

If you are deadly serious about doing well at your fishing, which let's face it we all are, I suggest that you concentrate on one venue and get to know it really well, this will give you a better chance of framing or getting a net of fish.

What's your choice of shock absorber through your pole? How much do you use and which strength for what species?

I use Garbolino Bazookarp CoEx hollow elastic for all of my carp fishing. It comes in a variety of sizes to cover all my needs when catching small F1s right up to large carp. I particularly like the orange size 16-20, the more you use it the better it becomes. I've had some in my top three kit for almost two years and it has become more stretchy and forgiving, perfect for catching all sizes of carp from 2lb to 20lb.

For my silver fishing I use Garbolino Solid LX which is pure latex and comes in No.3 to No.20, but I tend to use No.5 for all my silver fish work, just in case I hit a carp. This strength gives me the added control needed when playing a large fish using a puller system.

What gives you the edge when fishing, especially when fish are harder to catch?

I like to scale down the size of my hook and diameter of my line; I know from years of trial and error that it does make a difference. I see a lot of people come down to Whiteacres, which is known as a prolific water, and really struggle to catch fish because they are fishing far too heavy. On a good day you can get away with heavy gear, but when you think about it the fish on these commercial venues have seen it all and have now become very wary of thick lines and big hooks.

I would fish as light as 0.125mm Garbo Line and size 20 hooks for carp sometimes. As long as you use light elastic and let the fish run off you should have no problems. Having said that I always have a bagging rig ready in case the fish really switch on and have a go!

Another thing, which makes a difference, is having the float dotted down. Carp tend to feed by sucking in the bait and if they feel resistance they will blow the bait out again, which is why you have to fish dead depth.

Over the years you've fished a number of venues with great success. How do you keep up with the right methods? Or do you just do your own thing?

I've had my fair share of success, and if I had to say what makes the difference it is getting the basics right – which is correct feeding and presentation. I've always worked very hard at my fishing and never leave anything to chance, almost obsessive in my preparation.

To concentrate on one venue definitely gives you the edge, as does asking loads of questions and finding out what is the right approach. If somebody has done well, I make a point of asking them how they caught. It all goes in the memory bank for the next time.

What's the best match performance you've ever had?

I've been very lucky and won lots of matches – some small, some big. My best performance was in the Lancashire Winter League way back in 1996. I had just been asked to join Tri-Cast Highfield, which was a daunting experience as the team was full of big names. In those days team fishing was at its peak, we had 15 teams of 15 in the league that year and I was revved up to do well. I surpassed my expectations and helped Highfield to win the league and I won the individual title with five section wins and a second. We then went to the semi-final of the national competition on the

River Weaver where the team finished fourth and I won my section again. We qualified for the final on the River Trent and again I won my section and the team was crowned champions by two points to beat Dorking, one of the best teams in the land. That sequence of results gave me belief in myself and certainly got me more focused on my fishing.

Even good anglers can have bad days! Be honest… reveal your worst match and say why it went wrong.

I've had my fair share of disasters, I think everybody has! My worst match performances have probably been down to a combination of bad draws, bad decisions, bad fishing, bad timing… bad everything. I think to be more consistent in match fishing – and even pleasure fishing – it is down to better preparation and working hard during the session. Always give 100 per cent and never give up. I hate coming off the bank thinking I should have tried something. That really upsets me.

Harry's top ten match tips

1. Preparation for a match is paramount, make sure you have plenty of rigs and hooks tied, time spent in the water means more fish in the net.
2. Don't be afraid to scale down your hook and line size, especially when you're up against hard fished for commercial carp. They really are educated.
3. I prefer to take the number one sections out of my poles, this makes the pole even stiffer and allows the elastic to run more freely.
4. I use back shots, especially when its windy, as it makes control of the float infinitely better. There's nothing worse than a float being blown all over the place.
5. I often re-plumb my peg, just to check that the feeding carp haven't disturbed the silt on the bottom, and altered the depth fractionally.
6. Always ask plenty of questions, most anglers are more than happy to divulge information.
7. Get one step ahead of the fish. It's a rarity when you catch on the same method throughout a match, I normally have at least four areas of my peg primed, ready for a switch, when it goes quiet.
8. Keep an eye on what's going on around you. This can be the key to improving your catch rate, just by a simple change in method.
9. Try and find out about your peg off any venue regulars, or the owner of the fishery. It's amazing what a difference inside info can make.
10. Enjoy your fishing. It's amazing how many people get on a downer for the smallest of reasons.

7.8 Top ten barbel fishing tips

GARY NEWMAN* is one of England's best all-round big fish anglers. He has built up a wealth of knowledge about many species, including exotic species from all around the world. But one of his favourite fish close to home is the hard-fighting barbel, which has a growing popularity among UK and European anglers.

* Gary Newman's website is at www.garynewmanangling. com where you will find details of his fishing and coaching-guiding service

1. Hide your line

Barbel feed tight to the riverbed and if they come across your line it can spook them, so pinning everything down is a good idea. This can easily be done by using a coffin-shaped weight trapped between two float stops six foot [1.8m] or so above your main leger. You need to make sure the coffin weight is heavy enough not to lift off of the bottom or else it will waft around and be even more likely to spook the fish! On slower flowing

Gary with a 10lb 2oz River Kennet barbel.

Bait dropper – vital for good feeding.

rivers and when fishing close to the bank a four to six feet [1.2 to 1.8 metres] length of leadcore line with a piece of putty moulded around the leader knot can work well.

2. Don't ignore maggots

Barbel love maggots and at times can easily be caught on them. Unfortunately most other fish in the river also like these grubs! Maggots, and casters, work well in clear water conditions but often you will need to feed a lot of them to really get the barbel going and to feed off smaller fish. Often six to eight pints of bait will be required for a day's fishing. Feeding them via a bait dropper ensures they make it to the bottom, and introducing some hemp as well helps to draw the fish upstream to your bait. A bunch of six to eight maggots fished on the hook or hair-rigged can work very well.

Floods mean barbel – but also debris floating down the river!

3. Location

The most important thing is to find the fish, which makes them a lot easier to catch! These hotspots can vary depending on the time of year. Often, early in the season after spawning, the fish will be in very fast, shallow, well-oxygenated water such as weirpools and run-offs from them.

But as the season progresses they often drop lower down the stretch and can be found in areas with steady flow, clean gravel, and where there is cover such as snags or weed-beds. When the river is in flood, barbel will often be in spots out of the main flow and areas that normally wouldn't be worth fishing, such as cattle drinks or slacks, in the margins behind snags or any other obstruction that diverts the flow. In normal conditions these spots would be shallow or even dry land.

4. Don't be afraid of floods

A raging river can be enough to put many anglers off fishing, but so long as the water temperature is still warm enough the barbel will feed. In fact in winter it is often these coloured-water conditions, coinciding with a warmer spell, that are perfect for barbel fishing. A smelly offering such as spiced luncheon meat or boilie paste helps the fish to find the bait and you will often need a big lead to hold bottom and present a bait effectively. At times 8oz [225g] or more is needed. The first flood of the year is often best avoided as it brings a lot of rubbish down the river and makes it

Just some of the baits Gary loves for barbel fishing.

almost impossible to hold bottom with your gear. It is often best to wait for the floodwater to peak and start to drop. Barbel can also be caught on a rising river at times.

5. Stay mobile

On big rivers it can pay to stay in one spot and wait for the fish to move through your swim, but on smaller rivers roving is often the best approach. If there are barbel present in your swim then you'll often get a bite pretty quickly, or at least some indication such as line bites. If nothing has happened after an hour or so it is often worth a move along the river, maybe trickling a bit of bait into the spot so you can return later and see if any fish have moved

Gary Newman with a lovely 13lb 2oz barbel caught from the River Thames at night.

in. It can also pay to walk the stretch before you start fishing and bait a few spots. Then fish these areas in rotation, although this may not always be practical and depends on how many other anglers are around.

6. Fish at night

Barbel can be caught during the day but they often feed better after dark, when they are a lot more active. Around dusk they tend to move out of the snags or weed-beds where they might have spent the day and can cover quite large distances before returning to their usual haunts in the morning. You can catch the barbel as they move out or back into these areas – plus there is a chance of tempting one during the day from these swims. Darkness also means you'll catch them from more open areas where you wouldn't get bites during daylight. Riverbanks and even the waterways themselves are often a lot quieter at night, with fewer disturbances from humans, animals and boats, which also improves your chances of catching.

7. Avoid chub

Unfortunately chub like similar baits to barbel and often hooking one, especially in a confined swim, will spook everything else and you won't get another bite. Chub tend to give sharp rattles on the rod tip or quick plucks and then let go of the bait, as opposed to many barbel bites which are unmissable as the tip pulls round violently and just keeps going! You can certainly avoid a lot of chub by not striking at the smaller bites. Because of the way that chub feed, often taking a bait in their lips and moving off with it, they are far more susceptible to getting hooked on baits presented directly on the hook or on very short hairs. Increasing the length of your hair rig can often work and is still effective at hooking any barbel that takes your bait as they feed differently to the chub.

8. Pellets

Pellets account for a good proportion of the barbel that get caught and can be incredibly effective. Halibut pellets and similar are particularly good as the fish seem to like the taste of them, plus they leak off oil which creates a scent trail that can draw fish up to you from a long way downstream. Pellets are also very versatile and come in different shapes and sizes, meaning they can be loosefed by hand or catapult; fed by a bait-dropper; fished in open-end feeders plugged with groundbait; scalded and moulded around a Method feeder; or fished in PVA bags. They can also be soaked in other additives such as corn steep liquor and molasses. Pellets make a good hook-bait as

Flying back leads to keep line pinned to the bottom.

Squab bait with paste wrap-around – great to introduce a bit of feed and tempt barbel into your swim.

Isotopes to clip on your rod for night fishing.

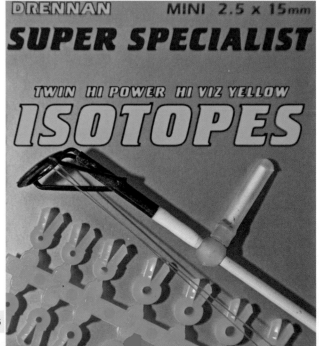

well, although they do start to breakdown after being immersed in water so need to be changed every hour or two depending on the water temperature.

9. Strong tackle

Barbel are one of the hardest fighting fish around and strong, balanced tackle is needed to land them. Usually a rod with a test curve between 1.5 lb [0.6kg] and 2 lb [0.9kg] is perfect, with the ones at the heavier end of the scale best suited to big rivers and casting heavy legers or feeders. If you're using a maggot approach or any smaller hook-bait presented on a size 12 or 14 hook you need a rod that has a nice through action

Be mobile and try a number of nice looking spots on smaller rivers.

otherwise you'll open out the hook, but the rod also needs enough power to be able to stop a fish getting into snags. I wouldn't normally go lighter than a 1.5 lb model. In most situations 10 lb [4.5kg] line is perfect and strong enough. A freerunner-style reel in the smaller sizes is ideal. This facility is useful if you get a bite when you happen to be looking away from the rod tip as it means you won't lose the rod!

10. Stick at it...

Good anglers catch big fish by working hard and putting in the hours. Of course some specimen fish are caught with a bit of luck but the most consistent big-fish anglers are the ones who work at getting things right… including being in the right place at the right time.

Chapter 8

Learning from Experts

Watching the world

Watching, asking questions and then fishing, are the best ways forward if you want to improve your angling ability. I've been lucky to fish with and watch some of the best anglers in the world and pick up some valuable tips along the way. Sometimes you don't realise what you have learnt – or it may be months or even years later that you put it into practice. The key to everything is that if you learn something is good – or bad – in certain conditions you must log that away in your brain for the future.

However, do not be put off if you watch a top angler and do not understand what they have done. Sometimes they adjust their tackle or what they are doing based on pure instinct. It's something that makes them a top angler – the same as a footballer blessed with natural ability that we would never, ever be able to compete with no matter how hard we train.

Here are just a few things I have learnt over the past 30-plus decades of watching some top match anglers…

Kevin Ashurst

Big Kev was undoubtedly one of the best-ever anglers to fish for England and, if nothing else, one look at his gear would teach you something… that you don't need the best looking tackle to catch fish! Kevin would have no hesitation in snapping his best float in two if he thought it wasn't up to the job he needed it for. He's even been known to bite the tip off a waggler so that it was just the right length! These are not world-class fishing tips but proof that you need the right gear for the job in hand…

When poles first arrived in the UK they were far too heavy to fish at the long lengths we do today. So Kevin decided that he would need to work out a bit in the gym – and this from a guy who was already no weakling.

When he won the World Champion's title in 1982 on the Newry Canal in Northern Ireland I was there… and I, like the others stood behind him, knew he was going to be the champion despite not getting a bite for quite a long time as others nearby caught.

It was a grim day fishing-wise but in the end you could sense Kevin would catch and slowly but surely he got a handful of small fish for less than 2 lb (900g) to take the title. Not a big catch at all but the way he put it together with skill and the delicate touch needed on the day was amazing.

He's still fishing, mostly in Ireland, where he has a home. He's also still winning…

Ian Heaps

Heapsy, World Champion in 1975, European Champion in 1985, a world gold team winner and former world match record holder, has a fishing brain that never stops working. No matter what the method or challenge Ian would work it out, often with his fellow north-westerner Kevin Ashurst.

Noted for his sliding float skills that won him the world title in Poland, Ian looks awkward when he casts with rod and reel – but I challenge you to put a float or a leger as accurately as he can!

Unlike many top anglers, he was never a slave to one method, one venue or tradition. Ian would learn anything and everything to keep up with the times.

On a trip to Germany Ian and I went into a local tackle shop for some advice after failing to catch on a practise session before a big match. The shop owner reached under the counter and handed us a tub with a red lid that contained brightly coloured, mostly red granules. He told us this stuff should be put into our groundbait and we would catch. This was before the days when additives and flavours hit the market big

time but sure as anything this gear turned our next session into a red letter day for bream.

A few months later, after we returned to England, a few anglers, and one in particular, started bagging up with fish on the River Trent. They were using something called Red Cap! If only we had been able to blag some more!

Another day we had to go and shoot pictures and put together words for a magazine feature but didn't know what subject to cover. Ian grabbed a few slices of bread from his kitchen, took me to a small farm pond close to where he then lived and blasted out roach like there was no tomorrow. Others were not getting bites – until he helped them out. He simply loves to see people catch.

Ian now runs his own fishery in south-west Wales. Needless to say he still catches, still wins matches and still helps others.

Dave Thomas

Anyone who was there will never, ever forget Dave Thomas winning both days of the World Championship when the event was held on the Warwickshire Avon.

The first day was the team match in those days and section winners qualified for the following day's individual match. The Leeds postal worker won the first day and the second despite the continentals giving most of the field a lesson in bloodworm fishing, groundbait and long poles.

But there was no way the visitors could live with the running line expertise of a man who had dominated results on the River Trent with his bronze maggot approach and was also crowned the first Matchman of the Year when matches had to contain more than 100 anglers to qualify for vital points.

The season he took the Matchman title, on the last day of the campaign, when Dave needed points to be sure of the trophy, I was pegged opposite him on the Rivers Tees – a venue he knew little about but one local to me. Needless to say he was second in the event and got the points that wrapped up the title. I was well happy to win my section that day – I might have done better if I hadn't kept glancing up to watch the master of the centrepin in action!

But what really stood out was when I followed him to the River Nidd to watch him in action at the start of the following season. Dave was continually moving his shot around his line as he ran a stick float through a lovely glide. He did it without even thinking… it was that natural to him. It was aimed at sorting out fish as they changed depth – and also to lure the bigger chub as they entered his swim. Only experience and ability can tell you when to do that. Until you have those things etched into your brain you have to experiment.

Will Raison

More than two decades ago, when I was part of the Farnborough AS side that dominated our local winter league, we turned up one Sunday morning to discover we were a man short. Think football team without a key player – only worse as everyone's result counts in a winter league. And starting with a zero points score because you are a man light could be a disaster. One of our leading lights was John Raison, who ran the commercial fishery Willow Park and now Gold Valley. With him was his early-teen son William, basically along for the ride.

Will had already started to win club matches and was proving a very capable angler but John was obviously reluctant to push his own son into the side. I, along with others in the team, said we had to give him a go. Armed with borrowed bits and pieces of tackle Will won his section for us. From then on – as they say – he never looked back.

His results with us catapulted him into the all-conquering Dorking side and then into the England set-up where he has been one of the side's most consistent scorers, leading up to his World individual win in 2008.

These days many of the country's 'name' anglers tend to specialise in one type of fishing but that tag could never be applied to Will who is a great all-rounder. He is a shining light to any young angler who wants to know if it is still possible to work your way through from the very bottom to the top.

Oh… and don't take him on at bowls. He's a bit good at that too!

Ivan Marks

For many, Ivan Marks was the anglers' angler. For me he was a fantastic character, someone with time for everyone who could have taught every single angler in the world something new.

Ivan's list of success in massive matches — and we are talking about times when some events had 1,000-plus entries — is far too big to print here. Good examples are his winning of the Great Ouse Championships in 1970, 1972 and 1973; numerous big events on the Welland, including the river's championships; and turning out 11 times for England.

I was lucky to share a cabin with Ivan at one of the earliest big matches on Ireland's River Erne — the Benson and Hedges. I was way out of my depth at the time, but by the end of the week the Leicester genius had my brain whirring with information about catching bream.

They were just simple things — like when to slip on a worm to catch a bream, twitching my hook-bait, how many casters to feed, why I should catch roach between the bream, when to switch end gear — but they were vital to my development as an angler.

It was unreal when he stood behind me in practice — not just because he was *the* great Ivan Marks — but because of how he *knew* when there was a bream in my swim. I swear he could talk telepathically with them!

Lots of sports stars talk of pressure. Ivan thrived on it! The more people behind him watching him in action the better. He played to the crowd and loved it. They loved him too.

Thankfully all of their eyes were on him when he was pegged next to me at Coombe Abbey Lake near Coventry for a big money invitation match. None of them saw me crack off my feeder rig as I attempted to cast as far as the master and with some sort of accuracy. That taught me the need for a shock leader.

Mind you, I still can't catapult out a ball of groundbait to distance and then cast a simple leger rig so my bait goes down the same hole — not without watching, which is just what he did as he talked to his fans. That was *total* class.

The world of fishing was robbed of a great character when Ivan passed away at the age of 67 in December 2004. Gone but his legacy will never be forgotten.

England's individual World Champions

Billy Lane 1963

Robin Harris 1969

Ian Heaps 1975

David Thomas 1981

Kevin Ashurst 1982

Dave Roper 1985

Tom Pickering 1989

Bob Nudd 1990, 1991, 1994, 1999

Alan Scotthorne 1996, 1997, 1998, 2003, 2007

Will Raison 2008

Sean Ashby 2012

Chapter 9

Weather Watch

Watch the weather! Cold or warm it could just be the right day to bag up with fish... if you read the conditions right.

Cloudy, warm with a good wind into your face will mean fish are feeding right in front of you.

Bright, sunny, few clouds, no ripple on the water surface means that the only place you are likely to catch is where there is cover for the fish to hide, like overhanging bushes and next to islands.

Sunny with some ripple on the water and you should be able to catch, although try floatfishing at different depths. Fish do not always live on the bottom!

Overcast, warm and with a nice ripple on the water is excellent. Make sure you are on the bank fishing! The weather is good for you and for the fish.

A few milder days in the middle of a really cold spell will usually encourage fish to start feeding, even if only for a short time.

Early and late in the day are always the best times for fishing in summer. In winter it could be too cold early in the day but just before it gets really cold, and just before dark falls, the fish could go on a feeding spree.

Many fish feed well in darkness but don't be surprised if they suddenly switch off and for a few hours in the middle of the night you can't get a bite.

The commonly held belief that fish feed better when it is raining is a load of rubbish! You must also take into account all of the factors outlined above.

Top weather tips

The very best weather conditions for fishing are:

- A falling barometer around 960 millibars

- Water temperature between 12 and 18°C (55-65°F)

- Air temperature 10-21°C (50-70°F)

- A south westerly breeze

- Cloud cover

Into winter...

The change from warmer to colder weather always brings patchy sport. Quite often it makes for very difficult fishing. But here are a few tips that could just save the day for you as summer turns to winter.

First, look for a period of settled weather. It doesn't matter if it's warm or cold, wet or dry, bright or cloudy. If you get three days where the weather is consistent the fish should be settled and feeding.

Don't be put off by a frost, unless it's the very first one of the winter and particularly harsh. It always takes time for frost to get through the water layers and cool it down – just like it takes time for the sun to warm up lakes and rivers at the start of the summer. And if a lake or river is carrying coloured water, worry about that frost even less, because the colour means it won't fish half as badly as a venue containing crystal clear water.

Scale down your tackle. Use thinner line and smaller hooks. You no longer need the heavy gear you used in summer as fish don't fight quite so strongly. But still don't take risks. Be sensible about tackle choice and remember you still have to land the fish even if you can attract bites.

If you are not getting bites, scale down hook size until you do. It's surprising what you can land on a good, strong size 20 or 22 hook!

Keep feeding but ease back on how much you put in. Once the feed is in the water you can't take it out! If the fish start to gobble up the grub you can always

Even in the worst of winter conditions fish will feed at some stage of the day, but probably only for a very short period.

step up how much groundbait or loose feed you offer them.

Groundbait in winter? Yes! Sometimes this can be the key to getting fish to feed. It is not the cold water swim killer many people used to believe. Just remember that it is an attractor, it should not feed. Ensure what you mix up hasn't got a heavy feed content.

Likewise, with water being a bit clearer choose a darker bait, often the darker the better. This creates a dark cloud or a dark layer on the bed of the lake or river which can give fish confidence to feed. It also means that your target fish are not so easily spotted by pike and other predators – like they would be if they were feeding over a bed of white or very light coloured groundbait.

The same baits you used in summer will work in winter but once again ease back on them.

Sweetcorn is no longer regarded as only a warm weather bait but you certainly don't want to be feeding much of it – in fact many top anglers feed no grains, sticking to the one on the hook in winter to lure fish. The bright yellow colour stands out great in clear water, or you can always use a food dye to make it red or black.

Bread really comes into its own in cold weather, flake and punch both scoring well when fish won't look at other baits.

Liquidise slices with their crusts removed through a food processor for feed. Throw in small balls of the bait, squeezed together lightly by hand, but be careful not to offer too much. You can spray on water if really necessary.

This is also the time when the day-saving bait can quite often be worms, both big or small. A single lobworm is deadly for big fish in still or flowing water. Redworms, dendrobaenas and smaller sections of worms will catch almost anything that swims.

Keep a selection of worm sizes to offer on the hook. But don't be tempted into thinking smaller baits are best on hard days. Quite often a larger worm will score where a small one has failed – fish can be tempted into being greedy!

TIPS

- Avoid bright, sunny days in winter, especially after a frost – unless you just fancy going into the countryside to enjoy the surroundings and have some peace and quiet.

- If the weather is overcast or the temperature has risen a few degrees then get on the bank!

- Cut back on loose feed and remember that small, natural baits are more likely to get you bites.

- Fish won't feed all of the time in the winter. But give them the right conditions and they will give you plenty of bites, even if just for an hour or two.

- Think carefully about your choice of swim or do a bit of homework and find out the areas where the fish have been caught by other anglers.

- Fish tend not to be spread out in the colder weather so there can be sections of lakes and rivers that are devoid of fish. When you do find where they are living for winter you can have a real red-letter day once they start to feed.

- Scale down line diameters and hook sizes compared to those you used in the warmer weather.

- Don't wear blinkers. There are times when all of the above guidance goes out of the window. Sometimes the fish won't care too much about the thickness of your line. And providing you have matched the size of hook to the size of bait you are using there won't be a problem.

- A nice big lump of bread flake or a whole juicy lobworm will often get you a bite when all of the smaller baits haven't even yielded a sniff.

- Experiment by chopping and changing tackle, presentation, feed and baits. In winter one little tweak can bring a bite.

Winter hot spots

Let's look at the hot spots (that's for catching fish rather than sitting in!).

It's natural for anglers to head for the deepest spots on a lake in winter but it's not always the best move! Shallower pegs warm up faster if there is a bit of sun, although deeper water can hold its heat longer in prolonged cold spells. And just because it's cold don't think the fish all go down to the bottom and hug

A big worm can be a deadly bait in all weather conditions.

the lakebed. They will, given the right conditions and feeding patterns, still come up in the water to feed.

The water is more than likely clearer than summer, so scale back on line diameter and hook size. Stillwater fish don't always fight as hard in winter and there is less weed about so you can afford to fish lighter.

Cover or no cover? Overhanging bushes and trees are always worth fishing near or under, but are not always the best spots in winter. They are good when it's bright and sunny as they offer shade, and sanctuary from predators. But open water heats up faster, and away from trees you won't have leaves that have fallen off the branches laying on the bottom, rotting away.

Some expert canal anglers taught me years ago that it is often best to fish totally exposed areas where there are no rotting leaves and no branches that stop heat getting to the water. Daft as it sounds, these can quite often be the best pegs on the very coldest of days.

In running water do you fish deep or shallow? Nice, steady glides with an average depth – say 5–7 feet (1.5–2 metres) – are good but never, ever ignore those fast shallows!

Fish action on a dull, cold day despite the lake peg being featureless on the surface. Plumb up to find the deep holes and ledges where fish could look for food.

Some of my best dace and chub catches in winter have come from water rushing through and with no more than two to three feet of depth.

Canals offer a great alternative for fishing in winter and nearly always produce. In fact nowadays with a lot less anglers on these venues they can be very productive.

Many stretches are now ignored by both pleasure and match anglers and it's like fishing a whole new venue – and with fish that have not only become less shy, but also grown quite a bit in size.

Never go fishing in winter without worms and bread. Bread is instant. If you are going to catch on the white stuff you normally get a bite pretty quickly. If it doesn't work quickly, don't be frightened to go back to it later in the day.

Worms are a must. All fish eat them and few can resist a few chopped up and dropped into your swim. They catch when all else fails.

And finally… if your time is restricted or you don't want to sit out all day in the cold for just a few bites, get yourself on the bank for the final hour or two of daylight. Swims that have failed to produce all day long can come alive as the light starts to fade. The fish become confident and ready to feed.

Ice work

Fishing through holes in the ice is fun and can offer some of the best sport of the winter!

But don't take risks. Stay on the bank and don't walk out onto ice that could easily smash and send you plummeting into very, very cold depths of water.

Get yourself a good ice-breaker and you are in business. I've got a big smash hammer on the end of a length of heavy-duty chain that is then fastened to a length of rope. The hammer is thrown high and long and smashes through some of the thickest ice. Then it is retrieved in a sawing motion so that the chain slices through the ice.

Create a long, narrow channel to fish into – not just a hole like you see Eskimos dropping their baits in! On canals this channel could stretch to the far bank. Excess ice can be scooped out with a landing net; gently shoved to the side, or under the remaining ice, using the cupping kit on a pole. Make sure that the pole can take the pressure, you don't want to break sections!

Place ice at the side of the hole that the wind is blowing towards. That way the breeze should still hit your piece of open water and help to stop it from freezing over again.

Don't worry about all the commotion, splashing and smashing. In fact make sure that your icebreaker hits the bottom and give it a good drag along the mud, gravel or whatever else is there. The disturbance can create a cloud, often containing natural foods. Fish do not appear unduly worried by the action. More often than not bites occur minutes after feeding the prepared swim.

Fishing is the same as normal. More than one area is baited, but very gingerly to begin – until you start to get bites. Bread punch with just a pigeon's egg-sized piece of liquidised is a good starting point. Chopped worm is another option. And on decent days even caster will work.

You will often start very cautiously and discover that in no time you are changing to pinkies because the fish are feeding better than you could even have imagined. Perch, roach and skimmers are the usual candidates through ice with gudgeon where they are present.

There's a theory that putting holes in the ice puts more oxygen in the water, in addition to the natural food your disturbance has caused.

Ice can actually mean hot sport. But never be tempted onto the ice, no matter how safe you might think it is!

Floods

Flooded rivers often see many anglers staying at home, or going to stillwaters and canals – which they may not really fancy fishing. But with careful planning it's still possible to grab some decent sport and enjoyable days out when rivers are raging through with extra water.

Extra water will mean extra colour to give fish more confidence in feeding. They are also swimming against stronger currents so will need more energy – by eating more food!

Fish will definitely move from their normal spots. Look for any slack water that could be stuffed with all sorts of species. Eddies, lock cuttings, the places where streams enter main rivers, even ditches that are usually dry but are now flooded. Moored boats also usually mean slacker water around them, or at least behind them.

Don't mess about with light gear. Get some weight under those floats, use a big leger or a swimfeeder with enough bait to get to the bottom. Baits with a bit of colour, or more important a bit of smell, will certainly work better.

A big fresh juicy lobworm, or a section of one, takes some beating in these conditions. It's usually possible to get away with using a nice stiff groundbait, either on its own of with a few samples of your hook baits.

And remember: when those floods die away and fast flowing waters start to slow down a little, the fishing should be excellent. The extra water will have washed away debris, fallen leaves and dying weed. And with a bit of colour in the rivers the fish will still have the confidence to feed freely at most times of the day.

Floods can be good in summer or winter but in the warmer weather the fishing can be exceptional if you choose carefully where you fish.

The best month...

September rates very highly for catching almost every species of fish that swims in European waters. It's probably down to a combination of weather and the approaching winter, but at any given time you have the potential for a great day's fishing.

Cold water lessons

When the weather is cold and horrible and you are struggling to catch, the best thing to do is scale down and fish smaller baits. Right? Wrong!

I always used to firmly believe that if you went down to a tiny 22 hook or smaller, tied on the thinnest trace in your box and slipped on a pinkie you were in for a bite. But I have since proven just how wrong that theory is.

First lesson: Pinkie is a good bait, especially fluoros, when the water is clear and cold. But sometimes when you can't catch on one you can get bites on doubles. In fact, dropping in a small ball of hard groundbait that breaks up slowly on the bottom also helps pull a few bites when fishing like this, often better than loose feeding a few grubs. Dark groundbait is best with each ball carrying just five or six pinkies.

Second lesson: Small worms are a great attractor. When they fail – even those nice little red ones or even when a bit of a big worm gets no enquiries – a big worm will do the business. Don't be afraid of using a

14, 12 or size 10 hook, depending on the size of the bait, and nip off the end of the worm.

Third lesson: Never, ever forget bread in colder weather. Don't just think that a tiny piece of bread created with a punch will tempt fish. Sometimes a big chunk of bread flake ripped from a loaf and squeezed onto your hook takes some beating. Think about it. Someone offers you a quick snack when you aren't really hungry – you can't be bothered. But they offer you a nice tasty morsel and your belly tells your brain take it. It's the same with punch or flake – one will work when the other doesn't.

Fourth lesson: Meat can be a lifesaver. It can work anytime of the year and virtually anywhere, in lumps from the size of a small pea up to almost golf ball-sized. Experiment. It's surprising how many times something different will actually work.

Hot sport in the heat

You will read elsewhere in this book how it is important to plumb accurately to find the depth of your swim. Many anglers fish their baits on or very near the bottom, as that is where most of their loose fed bait and groundbait will end up.

But sometimes, especially in warmer weather, the fish are not hugging the bed of the lake or river to feed. They will feed up in the water, often just below the surface. Many species, particularly carp, will come to the top searching for food and you can catch monster weights of fish. In fact on some hot, sunny days fishing just under the surface might be the only way you can catch.

Lovely grub. Liquidised bread.

It doesn't matter if the water is 4 feet (1 metre) or 16 feet (almost 5 metres) deep, at times those fish will come right up in the water, maybe to 3 feet (0.9 metres), but sometimes as shallow as 6 inches (15cm).

The key to catching is to get them to that level and keep them feeding with a constant stream of loose fed maggots, casters or pellets, or even some cloudy groundbait. Don't worry that some of that bait you feed through a pole pot – or more likely a catapult – falls to the bottom. The fish that find the bait on the bottom will also follow a steady trickle of bait to its source – the surface – as they hunt for more grub.

Feed them right and fish will go on a feeding frenzy, swirling on the surface.

Summer – and with coloured water and plenty of features it will be possible to catch despite the bright sun.

You might even see the fish swirling and splashing on the surface as they compete for your loose offerings. Don't feed any heavier, as you want them to stay there – heavier feeding could send them back to the bottom.

TIPS

- Constant little 'plops' caused by pellets hitting the water can attract fish like carp to investigate. They have become used to the noise on regularly fished waters and associate it with food.

- You can fish a pole float or a waggler with no shot down the line so your hook-bait falls slower and there is less likelihood of tangles.

- The best plan is to cast past your catching area, feed and then pull your float back among the fish in the feed area. Try casting just to the side of the feeding area or pulling the float your side of the fish, so that you catch fish that could be lurking just outside of the shoal. These are often the bigger fish.

- A big, dumpy waggler is often used for fishing pellets on the hook. This carries a lot of weight in its body so that it is easy to cast and lands with a splash that can attract the fish – who think it is bait arriving in the water.

- Don't strike at every sign on your float. Quite often the fish will brush against your line giving you a false bite. Takes when you are fishing like this are usually unmissable and often the fish hook themselves.

- If you lay your rod on a rest as your feed bait through a catapult, place it so that it's sideways on to the float, say around 45 degrees, so that a fish which hooks itself can bend into the rod and not snap you off easily. For the same reason do not engage the anti-reverse on your reel.

Chapter 10

Your Simple Reference Guide

Many manufacturers still refer to rods in feet and inches and pole in metres! Lines are often referred to in pounds and ounces breaking strains – but the length of line in metres! To help you through the confusion here are some easy metric-imperial conversion tables, and weight to diameter guides.

All weights and measures here are approximate and just a general guide. Different brands of line will have varying breaking strains for the same diameters. The only true way to get a measurement is with a micrometer. Some brands deliberately under-state the breaking strain of their lines to stay well inside legal limits. Smaller weights can vary fractionally – the same as stated weight carrying capacities of floats.

Lines

Normal nylon

Diameter	Breaking strain	
0.08mm	0.5kg	1lb 2oz
0.1mm	0.7kg	1lb 8oz
0.12mm	1kg	2lb 3oz
0.14mm	1.2kg	2lb 10z
0.15mm	1.4kg	3lb
0.16mm	1.6kg	3lb 8oz
0.17mm	2kg	4lb 6oz
0.18mm	2.1kg	4lb 10oz
0.2mm	2.4.kg	5lb 4oz
0.22mm	2.7kg	5lb 14oz
0.25kg	3.5kg	7lb 11oz

High tech/pre-stretched nylon

Diameter	Breaking strain	
0.06mm	0.37kg	12oz
0.07mm	0.43kg	1lb
0.08mm	0.81kg	1lb 12oz
0.09mm	0.96kg	2lb 2oz
0.1mm	1.2kg	2lb 10z
0.11mm	1.52kg	3lb 6oz
0.13mm	2.1kg	4lb 12oz
0.15mm	2.68kg	5lb 14oz
0.17mm	3kg	6lb12oz
0.19mm	3.3kg	7lb 6oz

Braid

Diameter	Breaking strain	
0.06mm	6kg	14lb
0.08mm	8kg	18lb
0.1mm	9kg	20lb

Weights

Shot weights

SSG – 1.6gm

AAA – 0.8gm

BB – 0.4gm

No. 1 – 0.03gm

No.3 – 0.25gm

No.4 – 0.2gm

No.5 – 0.15gm

No.6 – 0.1gm

No.8 – 0.06gm

No.9 – 0.05gm

No.10 – 0.04gm

No.11 – 0.03gm

No.12 – 0.02gm

Pole floats

A number of pole floats are marked with their weight carrying capacity – the table below shows these weights converted to shot sizes.

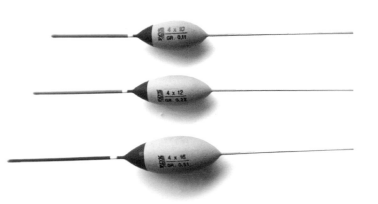

3 x 10 – 2 x No.10 shot

4 x 10 – 3 x No. 9 shot

4 x 12 – 5 x No.10 shot

4 x 14 – 6 x No.8 shot

4 x 16 – 8 x No.8 shot

4 x 18 – 3 x No.3 shot

4 x 20 – 4 x No.3 shot

5 x 20 – 5 x No.3 shot

6 x 20 – 4 x No.3 shot

EUROPEAN RECORDS

There are no official record fish lists for captures from mainland European waters but here are some that are generally recognised as being the best.

CARP

101lb 4oz (45.93kg) Euro Aqua, Nemesvita, Hungary

CATFISH (WELS)

297lb 9oz (134.97kg) River Po, Italy

CHUB

12lb 3oz (5.52kg) Vereinsgewasser, Germany

CRUCIAN CARP

8lb (3.64kg) Strossendorf, Germany

DACE

1lb 11oz (0.76kg) Attersee, Austria

EEL

13 lb 5 oz (6.04kg) Niepkuhle, Germany

GRASS CARP

89lb 5oz (40.5kg) River Danube, Hungary

IBERIAN BARBEL

34lb 3oz (15.5kg) Guadiana River, Spain

PERCH

8lb 4oz (3.75kg) Meuse River, Holland

PIKE

55lb 1oz (25kg) Grefeern Lake, Buhl, Germany

ROACH

5lb 12oz (2.62kg) River Weser, Germany

RUDD

5lb 15oz (2.7kg) River Weser, Germany

STURGEON

388lb (176kg) River Towy, Wales

ZANDER

41lb 4oz (18.7kg) River Danube, Austria

UK £16.99